Transforming Conflict through Insight examines the difficulties of conflict resolution and demonstrates how Bernard Lonergan's philosophy of insight can be applied to mediation to facilitate more productive and constructive negotiations. In this groundbreaking work, Kenneth R. Melchin and Cheryl A. Picard provide both an overview of conflict research and an introduction to Lonergan's 'insight theory.'

The volume discusses the different kinds of operations involved in learning and the role of feelings and values in shaping interactions with others. It also describes the practical experience of mediators who employ strategies of insight mediation for working creatively through conflict. Emphasizing the role of self-discovery and transformative learning in navigating conflicts, the authors show how insight and learning can move people past obstacles caused by feelings of threat.

Informative, compassionate, and convincingly argued, *Transforming Conflict through Insight* is a welcome resource for anyone working to resolve difficulties in an ethical and educational manner.

KENNETH R. MELCHIN is a Professor of Ethics in the Faculty of Theology and Director of the Lonergan Centre at Saint Paul University, Ottawa, and member of the Faculty of Graduate Studies and Research at the University of Ottawa. He is the author of many books and articles. His most popular book, *Living with Other People*, has been published in English, French, and Spanish. Over his long and distinguished scholarly career, he has also participated in numerous community projects in the fields of conflict resolution and community economic development. In 2002 Dr Melchin was awarded the Government of Canada's International Year of Volunteers Award.

CHERYL A. PICARD is Associate Professor in the Department of Law and Director of the Centre for Conflict Education and Research at Carleton University in Ottawa. She has been involved in conflict resolution and mediation work for over thirty years in Canada, the United States, Europe, Cuba, and Bermuda. In 2008, Dr Picard was recognized for her longstanding peace work by the Department of Peace Initiative in cooperation with the Canadian Voice of Women for Peace and the Civilian Peace Service Canada. She also received Family Mediation Canada's prestigious FAMMA Award for exceptional contributions to the field of mediation. This is Dr Picard's third published book on the topic of mediation.

KENNETH R. MELCHIN AND
CHERYL A. PICARD

Transforming Conflict
through Insight

UNIVERSITY OF TORONTO PRESS
Toronto Buffalo London

© University of Toronto Press Incorporated 2008
Toronto Buffalo London
www.utppublishing.com
Printed in Canada

Reprinted in paperback 2009

ISBN 978-0-8020-9175-8 (cloth)
ISBN 978-1-4426-1051-4 (paper)

Printed on acid-free paper

Library and Archives Canada Cataloguing in Publication

Melchin, Kenneth R., 1949–
   Transforming conflict through insight / Kenneth R. Melchin and Cheryl A.
Picard.

   Includes bibliographical references and index.
   ISBN 978-0-8020-9175-8 (bound). –ISBN 978-1-4426-1051-4 (pbk.)

   1. Conflict management. I. Picard, Cheryl Ann II. Title.

   HM1126.M45 2008   303.6′9   C2008-902990-9

This book has been published with the help of a grant from the Canadian
Federation for the Humanities and Social Sciences, through the Aid to
Scholarly Publications Programme, using funds provided by the Social Sci-
ences and Humanities Research Council of Canada.

University of Toronto Press acknowledges the finanical assistance to its
publishing program of the Canada Council for the Arts and the Ontario
Arts Council.

University of Toronto Press acknowledges the financial support for its publishing activities of the Government of Canada through the Book Publishing Industry Development Program (BPIDP).

Jacket photograph courtesy of iStockphoto

This book is dedicated to conflict resolution practitioners and scholars who help parties gain insights that reshape feelings and transform conflicts.

Contents

Acknowledgments

It has long been our dream to collaborate on a book: a book that combined our diverse yet complementary strengths and interests. This book is the realization of that dream. It began amidst conversations in the Lonergan Reading Group at Saint Paul University, 2004–5, and we wish to express our gratitude for the wonderful contributions of our friends and colleagues who participated in those sessions: Lorraine Berzins, Derek Bianchi Melchin, Danny Lyonnais, Teresa Janz, Darlene O'Leary, Morag McConville, Neil Sargent, Robert Sauvé, Elizabeth Sterritt, and Germain Zongo. We owe a particular debt of gratitude to Danny, Teresa, and Morag who in 2001–2 worked with us to produce and analyse the 'Danny and Teresa' mediation video that led to the Insight Mediation approach.

Between 2005 and 2008, the book advanced beyond anything we could have envisioned in the early stages of writing. Many of the insights developed along the way arose with the help of conversations with colleagues and friends, and we wish to express our gratitude to the students, mediators, coaches, mentors, and faculty in the Graduate Certificate in Conflict Resolution program at Carleton University, and to all our colleagues at the Centre for Conflict Education and Research in the Department of Law at Carleton, the Lonergan Centre at Saint Paul University, the Faculty of Theology at Saint Paul, the Lonergan Workshop at Boston College, the Insight Peace and Conflict Group, the Symposium on Conflict Resolution held annually in Ottawa, the Sargent Shriver Peace Institute, and the Institute for Conflict Analysis and Resolution at George Mason University, Washington, DC. Particular thanks go out to Andrea Bartoli, Jamie Price, and Neil Sargent who read drafts of texts on Insight Mediation, provided encouragement, and helped clarify ideas.

We are grateful to Darlene O'Leary whose research on learning theories and Lonergan contributed to chapters 1 and 3, to Derek Bianchi Melchin whose research on conflict theories contributed to chapter 2, to Lorraine Berzins at the Church Council on Justice and Corrections whose help in selecting and analysing the two case studies contributed to chapter 5, to Pierre LaViolette, Morag McConville, and Josh Daly who contributed to editing and preparing the index and final manuscript, and to Morag McConville at the Lonergan Centre at Saint Paul University whose research and organizational skills helped make things happen along the way. Of course, we accept responsibility for the final form of the text. We thank the Research Centre and the Administration at Saint Paul University for support services for research contributing to this book.

We wish to thank Fred Lawrence, Director of the Lonergan Institute at Boston College, for the opportunity to present and receive feedback on early versions of materials for chapters 4 and 5 at the Lonergan Workshop, 2002, 2005, and 2007. We wish to thank the editor of *Catholic Theological Society of America, Proceedings* for permission to reprint selected passages from 'Reaching Toward Democracy: Theology and Theory When Talk Turns to War,' *Catholic Theological Society of America, Proceedings* 58 (2003): 41–59, by Kenneth R. Melchin, © Catholic Theological Society of America.

Finally, and most important, we wish to thank our partners, Chick and Sandie. You have been friends and companions at every step along the way of this journey, and we could not have done it without your encouragement and support.

Research for this book was carried out with the aid of a grant from the Social Sciences and Humanities Research Council of Canada, 2004–7. This volume was published with the aid of a grant from the Aid to Scholarly Publications Program of the Canadian Federation for the Humanities and Social Sciences.

TRANSFORMING CONFLICT THROUGH INSIGHT

1 Conflict and Insight: Setting the Stage

This book is about conflict. There can be no doubt that conflict is on our minds. It is not only a topic; it is our very mode of access to topics of public interest. Media reports focus on conflict, and they bring us the events of the day by probing disagreements, clashing ideas, and warring factions. Our privileged mode of public discourse is debate. We think of social and political life as saturated with difference and dissension. As citizens, we are drawn into this scenario, not simply as observers, but as participants charged with the task of thinking and working through the challenges of conflict.

Faced with this media portrait, what do we expect of ourselves? What do we assume about conflict, and what do we think we can do about it? As citizens of democracies, we have ideas about conflict that are bound up with theories of democratic life. We expect pluralism and toleration. Democracies must welcome women and men from diverse and conflicting religious, cultural, and philosophical traditions. We expect to interact with others who hold conflicting values and convictions, and all of this requires something of us. Yet we also expect our political and justice institutions to intervene on our behalf when conflicts get out of hand. We expect law, order, and defence against threat. We expect political institutions to assure our liberty and equality. Still, democratic institutions do not work mechanically, nor do we look favourably upon the heavy-handed imposition of force. Our institutions of politics and justice work well when they gather and focus the will of citizens, and conflicts hamper this work of gathering and focusing. So how do we support our institutions in their work? What does conflict require of us as citizens?

Our interest in this book is in exploring a novel line of reflection on conflict. We believe we are witnessing a heightened awareness of citizen participation in dealing with the conflicts of public life, and we want to know how this participation can make a difference for the better. To help answer this question, we propose an analysis that focuses on conflict as *learning*.

Conflict is a normal part of life, and often it is resolved without great difficulty. While media reports focus on the big conflicts, the ones that seem beyond us, daily life provides evidence of countless conflicts that we handle fairly well. Our interest is in exploring the learning that goes on in these ordinary cases. Whether we deal with issues ourselves or turn to third parties for assistance, resolving conflicts leaves us changed in subtle but important ways. Embroiled in conflict, we are adamant, we are intransigent, we are fearful, we are focused, and we oscillate between fight and flight. But as issues get resolved, our attitudes and feelings give way. We become more open, more curious, we engage with others, and feel the freedom to explore avenues that previously were closed. This change is a transformation in us, and our interest is in exploring this transformation as a form of learning.

In the chapters that follow, we explore how conflict resolution can be understood as learning. To be sure, this is not the learning of classrooms and textbooks. Nor is it helpful to conjure up images of scolding teachers or magisterial lectures. The learning we experience in conflict is more like the learning involved in skill development, personal growth, healthy relationships, or innovation. It involves insight, discovery, and the shifts in feelings, perspectives, and relationships that accompany these experiences. Exploring this transformation as learning provides novel insights into conflict resolution: insights that can prove helpful in dealing with the more difficult conflicts of our lives.

Our principal resource guiding this novel line of reflection is the Insight Theory of Canadian philosopher Bernard Lonergan.[1] More than any other philosopher or social scientist, Lonergan has focused on understanding acts of insight. His analyses are rich and complex, and have been found relevant to diverse fields of experience.[2] Insights are curious and elusive, and they stubbornly resist careful analysis. They have an odd structure to them. Probing this structure invites us into a different way of thinking about conflict. Insights come in different types, each with its own distinctive contribution to the learning process. They affect our cognition as well as our feelings, attitudes, values, and relationships. They are deeply personal, yet they occur in social contexts, and their import is profoundly social. Lonergan's work provides a subtle and profound analysis of insight, and we draw on this analysis to explore the transformative learning that goes on in conflict.

We offer the analyses of these chapters as a contribution to the study of conflict. Since the 1970s and 1980s, conflict studies has emerged as a field of theory and practice dedicated to probing the mysteries of conflict and developing ways of living conflict more humanely. We believe that understanding conflict as learning offers an important perspective to the field, and Lonergan's Insight Theory brings a wealth of resources to this line of analysis. We address the chapters, first and foremost, to theorists, practitioners, and students of conflict. Yet we believe our reflections may also have a wider appeal – to Lonergan scholars interested in applications of his thought; and to women and men struggling to understand their lives as citizens amidst the conflicts of public life.

This focus on conflict, learning, and insight sets the itinerary of the book. In chapter 2 we begin by situating our line of inquiry within an overview of the history of conflict studies. We trace the theme of learning that emerges through this history, and show how Insight Theory carries forward some important developments in the field. In chapter 3 we introduce Lonergan's Insight Theory. We focus on the method of self-understanding, the role of experience and questioning in learning, direct and inverse insights, verification, and feelings and values. Throughout the discussions, we begin exploring some of the rich resources Insight Theory offers to the understanding of conflict.

The introduction to Insight Theory sets the groundwork for the chapters that follow. The relevance of Lonergan's work to conflict studies is not simply a fanciful notion; it is a line of theory that has been tested in practice and in the training of conflict mediators. This has led to the development of the Insight Mediation Model at Carleton University, Ottawa. We set out some of the major features of this model in chapter 4, and explore how Insight Theory provides novel insights into the work of mediators. In chapter 5 we examine how Insight Theory can prove helpful in understanding the role of alternative dispute resolution measures within the criminal justice system. We examine two case studies that illustrate the role of insight and learning in the transformations that occur when alternative justice measures prove successful. We believe that understanding insight can help clarify both the challenges and the values of such justice processes. Finally, in chapter 6, we offer some concluding reflections on Insight Theory and our role as citizens in the conflicts of democratic life. Our focus throughout the chapters is on everyday conflict and not the complex conflicts of international violence, war, or genocide. Our hope is that lessons learned from simpler cases may prove helpful in future research on more difficult conflicts.

To introduce the line of inquiry of this book, we begin with three snapshots. The first snapshot touches on everyday conflicts, the second on how we expect the justice system to deal with conflicts, and the third on how conflict shapes ideas about democratic life. In each, we observe two contrasting perspectives, two different ways of thinking about conflict and how it is to be resolved. Our discussion focuses on different assumptions we carry with us in thinking about conflict. In particular, our interest is in assumptions about our role as participants in resolving conflicts and the role of learning in this process.

Conflict is common in our lives, yet we do not reflect often on our assumptions about conflict. These assumptions shape expectations about our roles and responsibilities in family, neighbourhood, workplace, and civic life. More than this, our assumptions about conflict shape ideas about what we expect to happen in resolving conflict. Whether we go through the courts or use more informal processes, resolving conflict leaves us changed in subtle but important ways. This change involves an element of learning. Our goal in this book is exploring how Insight Theory can contribute to the study of conflict by understanding the transformative learning that occurs when we navigate successfully through the conflicts of our lives.

Snapshot #1: Everyday Conflict

The first snapshot involves everyday conflicts, and the ideas portrayed are both common and familiar. The conversation is between two approaches towards the role of third parties in conflicts. When we cannot handle conflicts ourselves, we often look to third parties to intervene, and they can act either as adjudicators or mediators. Adjudicators decide on the dispute, while mediators help the parties themselves work out a solution. A brief examination of each sheds light on some interesting assumptions we carry with us in our relations with family and friends, neighbours and coworkers.

Many conflicts are handled quite easily, but when we run into problems, we often look for someone to decide who is right and who is wrong about the issue. She might be a parent or an elder, he might be a leader in the community or an expert in the field, or she might hold the role of supervisor or manager if the conflict is in an organizational setting. Someone with the authority to settle the matter for us is called an adjudicator, and adjudication is one of the most familiar forms of conflict resolution. Obvious examples involve courtroom judges and municipal board adjudicators.[3] What distinguishes adjudication is the adjudicator's role in resolving the conflict. Adjudicators are third parties who make decisions on conflicts in the light of known rules or procedures that are generally accepted by parties. Often the process takes place in formal settings, and often it involves professionals like lawyers representing the parties. Typically the process focuses on matters of law or policy, and to be adjudicated, the issues must be defined in narrow, precise terms. Getting a resolution means getting an authoritative ruling on how the rules apply to the case.

An important feature of adjudication is that resolving the particular dispute is often not the only aim of the process because adjudicators must consider cases, not simply on their own terms, but also as precedents for future conflicts. Consequently, cases often are treated as types rather than strictly as of particular importance to the people involved. Disputants often play a limited role in adjudications, and proceedings frequently unfold in an adversarial and highly regimented environment. Adjudicators' rulings determine the winners and losers, and normally the parties go into the process expecting to abide by the ruling.

The second process in the snapshot is mediation.[4] Mediation is quite different from adjudication; in fact, it is an alternative to adjudication often referred to as an alternative dispute resolution (ADR) process. Mediation is generally understood to be more flexible and more user-friendly. It is used in an extremely wide variety of contexts, from families in remote villages, to commercial boardrooms, and international theatres of war and diplomacy. While mediation takes many diverse forms, it is typically understood to be a consensual process in which an impartial third party plays an active role in helping disputants themselves work out mutually acceptable solutions. In contrast to adjudication, mediators do not make decisions.

What distinguishes mediation is the interaction between the parties and the active role they play in achieving outcomes. Mediators have no authority to impose decisions, and even when mediation is mandated by courts, outcomes must receive the consent of the parties. Mediators do their work by facilitating communication between parties. This can involve helping clarify issues and beliefs, exploring relationships, modelling good communication, probing for underlying assumptions and interests, helping overcome obstacles, and charting paths towards consensual outcomes. Mediations are highly participatory, they aim at mutually agreeable outcomes, and because they need not be precedent-setting, they can focus intensely on the full range of details and needs that participants find relevant to this particular conflict.

Clearly, one of the differences between the two processes is the form and focus of participant involvement. The main work of adjudications is done by professionals or authority figures, and their work is to determine outcomes. Their formality is linked to their function. Their focus is on individual cases, but only in the light of policy or law and its consequences for institutions and the publics they serve. In mediation, the disputants are the principal actors and the conflict at hand is the concern of the process. The result is that mediations can focus on personal relationships. Mediations are not conducted in public, and this accords them the liberty to involve participants much more intimately in exploring the particular needs and personal relations of the conflict. Some mediations do function within legal contexts, and in these cases, mediators and legal counsel determine the legal boundaries related to the dispute. Once this is done, however, the parties can focus on the issues that matter to them. They do the work of resolving the conflict, and in one way or another, this involves enough of a focus on their relationship to enable the move to resolution.

Of particular interest to us is the transformation that occurs to move parties from being stuck in conflict to reaching solutions. In both adjudication and mediation, parties enter in a state of conflict and leave with some form of resolution. The resolution may involve the parties' wholehearted agreement, or it may involve little more than a grudging willingness to comply with an adjudicator's ruling.[5] Our interest is in exploring this transformation, and our particular focus is on the learning involved in the process. Both adjudication and mediation involve learning, and in both cases, the learning plays an important role in determining outcomes. No doubt, this is not the learning of classrooms or textbooks. But it is learning nonetheless. It may involve the dramatic discovery of new ways forward, or merely the bleak realization that we must indeed accept our fate. In both cases we learn something, and this learning is decisive for the conflict.

In adjudication, most of the learning is done by adjudicators themselves. The conflict is resolved when they learn enough about the case and its relationship to the law or policy that they can interpret it and apply it to the case. Their judgments are the culmination of this learning.[6] The role of disputants is to accept the ruling of adjudicators. This can involve significant learning but it need not. Minimally, adjudication asks participants to do little more than accept what is required for compliance.

With mediation the story is quite different. It is the parties themselves who must work out solutions. Mediation requires participants to become intimately involved in learning, and their learning is decisive for the outcome. This can involve simple things like learning fair options for dividing contested amounts of money. But it often involves more difficult learning about things like motivations, cares and threats, relationships and values. Mediators play a role in this learning but their goal is not diagnosing conflicts or determining results; it is facilitating disputants' own learning. It is the disputants themselves who do the work in mediation, and the work they do requires enough learning to move them from adversity to agreement.

Snapshot #2: Conflict and Justice

The second snapshot focuses on the conflicts that bring citizens into the orbit of the criminal justice system. The conversation here is between the retributive and restorative models of justice. To be sure, crimes are quite different from interpersonal conflicts. In fact, we feel a certain reluctance to call crimes conflicts at all. They lack the symmetry, the balance of other conflicts, the assumption that both parties have legitimate claims. Crimes involve right and wrong, they are offenses, and offenders must be caught, tried, and dealt with. Still, there is a profound sense in which the actions of offenders are in conflict with the good of victims and society. This is why they are called crimes. It is this conflict that is central to the very meaning of crime. Victims feel this conflict most intensely. Crimes are conflicts writ large.

In the retributive model,[7] crimes are understood to conflict with the good of society. Crime is a breach of society's laws and the objective of justice is to establish guilt and restore social balance by punishing offenders. While crimes typically involve victims and offenders, this model does not focus on this relationship. Rather, crimes are against the good of society as a whole. Obeying society's laws is each citizen's responsibility for carrying his or her share of the burden of social life. In return, we all enjoy society's benefits. When one person violates these laws, their crime brings them into conflict with us all. Consequently, it is the state that must exact justice on behalf of all.

Retributive justice must also perform the function of deterrence. When crimes are punished, the assumption is that both actual and potential offenders are deterred from resorting to future crimes. Consequently, penalties must speak loudly and clearly to the whole of society that crime does not pay. The work of justice is done by professionals working on behalf of the state; their job is to determine guilt and impose penalties proportionate to the harm done, and the process is formal and impersonal.

In the restorative justice model,[8] crime is understood differently. Here the focus is on society as a web of relationships, and criminal acts are in conflict with the good of these relations. The object of justice is to repair harm to the victim and community, restore social relations, and integrate offenders into community life. The result is that punishment is not automatically understood as the best response to crime. The work of justice involves finding appropriate responses that achieve the restoration of victim, offender, and community relations. This work can never be achieved purely formally, and it cannot be done entirely by professionals acting on our behalf. It requires the meaningful participation of victims, offenders, and community members. It needs a less adversarial environment to work well, and in this model, the best defence is not achieved principally by deterrence, but by nurturing and restoring social relations. Justice, here, is healing the social wounds caused by criminal conflict. It belongs to the community, and its achievement requires the active participation of all.

In this conversation, we observe how the two models understand justice differently, how these notions of justice are linked to ideas about conflict, and how the two models involve citizens and the state differently in achieving justice. In the retributive model, crime is in conflict with the good of society as a whole, and so justice is achieved by the state. Citizens, for the most part, do not act directly in the system. Rather, the state acts on our behalf, and this work is done by professionals. This is the case for offenders, but it is also the case for victims. In the restorative model, we see a very different picture. Here, crime is in conflict with the webs of relations that make up society, and these relationships implicate citizens personally. The result is that achieving justice requires the active involvement of victims, offenders, and communities.

Finally, as in the previous snapshot, we observe how the two models involve important assumptions about learning. In the retributive model, justice is achieved through the learning of justice professionals. For the most part, the learning of victims, offenders, and citizens is restricted to the learning of compliance. This may not be insignificant, and the social import of this form of learning may well be more profound than we have imagined.[9] Still, what is important here is the learning involved in determining outcomes.

In the restorative model, citizens' involvement in learning is more personally linked to outcomes. Sentences involve much more than simply prescribing jail terms. They need to be worked out to meet the needs of offenders, victims, and communities. This can engage judges, lawyers, parole officers, social workers, and community members in considerable learning. Repairing harm to victims, particularly when they have been traumatized by crime, can require intensive learning to overcome fear and rebuild trust. Restoring social relations can involve community members managing fear and getting past stereotypical images of offenders. This can require some hard learning. Finally, habilitating or rehabilitating offenders can require the long roads of learning that take them out of lives of poverty, abuse, violence, and despair into new-found hope in themselves and their community. In both models, the meaning of justice is linked to ideas about conflict, and its resolution is linked to assumptions about learning.

Snapshot #3: Conflict and Democracy

The third snapshot is a conversation about democracy and the role of conflict in democratic life. Public figures tend to speak of democracy with clarity and conviction. They leave us with the impression that we all understand what democracy is and what it involves. The fact is, however, there are quite different ways of understanding democracy, and many of the differences revolve around diverse ideas about conflict. The two portraits of democracy represented here reflect ideas and convictions we all share to some degree. Yet they are different, and the differences reach back to echo the philosophies of two founding fathers of democracy, Thomas Hobbes and Jean-Jacques Rousseau.[10]

Typically, we think of democracy as a political system, a system of government whose natural home is the nation state. Its principal goal is securing the freedom of citizens, and the signs we usually look for are things like free elections, free political parties, free speech, and free markets.[11] The image that often comes to mind is Hobbes's portrait of an aggregate of citizens, all of us endowed individually with natural rights and freedom to determine our own living, but who find ourselves in a state of perpetual strife because our plans invariably conflict with those of our neighbours. We solve this problem democratically when we enter into a social contract to hand over some of our natural rights to the state. The state exercises them on our behalf to protect our freedom from the intrusion of others and resolve the conflicts that arise from our differences.[12] Justice is achieved when state institutions do their job handling conflict and securing a space for citizens to live their individual lives in freedom.

Philosophers such as Rousseau developed a somewhat different approach, one that focuses on citizens' participation as the goal of democratic life.[13] In this second portrait, the basic state of society is conceived, not as one of perpetual strife among individuals, but as one where we live within traditions and communities of shared interests and values.[14] Democracy, in this view, is the more wide-ranging, participatory enterprise of citizens, not primarily an activity of the nation state. When society is democratic, the projects and policies of public life are constructed with the free and equal participation of citizens. When conflicts arise, they are resolved collectively by appealing to this lived tradition and the shared values of communal life. Justice is secured when the state assures the full, free, and equal participation of all.[15]

Once again, we observe two different approaches to the role of conflict in social life. In the Hobbesian approach, the goal of democracy is freedom, but freedom invariably means conflict. We all hold our own personal values and convictions, and the assumption is that none of us is about to change our convictions to suit someone else. These differences must be tolerated equally by others. Our values are there; they are our right. But the result is they invariably create conflict. We cannot squash this conflict by demanding compliance with any particular view of life. This would be antidemocratic. So, when things get out of hand, we have to deal with this conflict. Democracy is achieved when the state enters to manage these conflicts on our behalf through the laws and institutions of the political and justice systems.

The Rousseau approach, on the other hand, makes different assumptions about conflict. In spite of our differences, we are also connected. We are connected by our traditions and institutions, we are connected by the projects that bring us together in day-to-day life, and we are connected by a shared commitment to full and equal participation in building public life together. These connections are what we draw on when we face conflicts. The result is that this portrait focuses on the conflicts that citizens can indeed resolve, either individually or with the help of various social agencies. The state's role in democracy, then, is to assure that this activity is fair and open to the equal participation of all.

As in the previous snapshots, the two approaches reveal interesting assumptions about learning. In the Hobbesian portrait, the focus is on intractable conflicts because they are the threats to our freedom and security. We regard these conflicts as intractable because we assume other persons are intractable. We think of them as unable to learn, unable to shift their own course to make room for ours. In this portrait, we are obliged to apply the same assumption to ourselves. For either of us to move from our positions would require some form of learning, some shift in our positions in which we learned something from our interactions with others. The Hobbesian approach is pessimistic in its assumptions about this interpersonal learning, and this is why it focuses so strongly on state institutions. The principal learning for resolving conflicts here is done by state authorities, and the minimal learning required of citizens is the learning of compliance.

The Rousseau portrait is different. The accent here is on shared traditions, interaction, cooperation, and the conflicts we can resolve together. All of these entail learning. Most important is the learning that occurs when we draw on shared resources to resolve conflicts. This involves the vigorous engagement of citizens, and in this model, this engagement is at the centre of what democratic life is all about. These assumptions about learning and conflict play a key role in the Rousseau model, and they highlight the way that ideas about democracy are integrally bound up with assumptions about conflict and learning.[16]

Conflict, Participation, and Learning

Our selection of conversation partners in each snapshot has not been arbitrary. In each, we observe a more traditional approach and an alternative approach. For generations, our ideas about conflict, justice, and democracy have been shaped by traditional images of adjudicators, courts, and parliaments. We have relied on their professional competence to act on our behalf, they have stamped our habits of thinking and feeling, and they continue to dominate media reports of public events. At the same time, we are watching the entry of alternative approaches that both reflect and shape our ideas about society and politics. The last few decades have witnessed the entry of mediators, advocates of restorative justice, and theorists of participatory democracy. What characterizes these alternatives is their focus on the heightened participation of citizens in shaping the direction of social life.

To be sure, we have not greeted the alternatives with unqualified enthusiasm. There can be no question of replacing all our traditional institutions. Nor are we all that sanguine about interacting intensely with each other as citizens. We are different, and we are cautious about our differences. The more we become involved, the more we realize that citizen participation is fraught with ambiguities. We do know, however, that dramatic changes are occurring in society, and wrestling with these changes calls us to involvement in social life in new ways.

Our assumption through the following pages is that the proliferation of alternative approaches signals a direction towards greater citizen participation in public life. We are coming to believe that the direction of society cannot be left entirely to professionals or elected officials.[17] Citizens can and should be involved in wrestling with the conflicts at the heart of social and political affairs. Moreover, these ideas about citizen participation are not restricted to the alternative approaches. They are shaping the way we participate in more traditional institutions. In the wake of the scandals that have rocked public life, we feel reluctant to leave politics to the politicians. Nor do we hesitate to criticize adjudicators and judges when they bring down rulings we feel are wrong. More and more, we find ourselves drawn into public affairs, not simply to elect representatives and comply with their rulings, but to engage in the deliberation itself. The problems and challenges are too big to be left only to professionals. We no longer instruct our children to be seen and not heard; we teach them to inquire, discuss, challenge, and debate. All of this reflects a growing awareness of the role of citizen participation in public life. This does not rule out traditional institutions, nor does it preclude apathy. What it does mean is that we are united in our scrutiny of institutions and our criticism of apathy.

One way or another, citizen participation has captured our attention. In the decades to come, we will observe the proliferation of alternative initiatives, and we will be drawn into traditional institutions in new ways. But what will this require of us? How can we do this work well? We believe our assumptions about conflict and learning need to be examined and questioned if we are to rise to the challenges posed by this participation in public life. Our goal in the following chapters is to explore some of these assumptions and questions. In particular, our interest is in conflict. Why has conflict become so prevalent in our lives? What kind of learning goes on when we wrestle with conflict? How can learning about learning help us work through our conflicts more effectively?

The Growing Interest in Conflict

The rising attention to conflict in our lives is breathtaking. Books on conflict fill libraries, and discussions of conflict crowd the airwaves. Is conflict a new thing? We suggest that while conflict is not new, our attention to it has taken a new form, and there are a number of reasons for this.

One of the most prominent is international affairs. The twentieth century witnessed some of the most violent conflicts ever experienced by humanity. The two wars of the first half-century ravaged the planet. Then, for four decades following the Second World War, East-West tensions fuelled a nuclear arms race that threatened the future of humanity. The end of the Soviet era seemed to promise a period of peace, but this hope was soon shattered by diverse conflicts erupting worldwide: in the former Yugoslavia, Somalia, Rwanda, Iraq, Haiti, Afghanistan, and Sudan, to name a few. The experience of the 11 September 2001 attacks on the World Trade Center and the Pentagon and the wars in Iraq and Afghanistan ushered in an era that brought the spectre of violent conflict much closer to home for North Americans.

On the environmental front, growing public awareness of climate change and the limits to the planet's carrying capacity have heightened concerns over the very possibility of future life on earth. Conflict will invariably accompany the efforts of growing populations to live with dwindling resources amidst tumultuous and devastating environmental change. There can be no doubt that the future promises extraordinary challenges, and working through the conflicts arising throughout these challenges is now regarded as the lot of present and future generations.

Another reason is multiculturalism. In the second half of the twentieth century, our cities and neighbourhoods became much more culturally diverse than they had been; so much so that we have begun to ask whether we need to think of our national identities differently. In Canada, this has given rise to a vigorous public debate. Instead of expecting new Canadians to fit in, public figures now celebrate the diversity they bring to this country's cultural mosaic. It is now common to speak of Canadian culture as multicultural. The result is a growing concern about how we will live cultural diversity, and debates about cultural diversity are now widespread worldwide. Diversity means conflict, but it also means citizens need to handle conflict differently. In multicultural societies citizens can no longer approach conflicts with the common convictions and values of shared traditions. Now citizens are not sure what they will find to agree upon. The result is that conflict has become the focus of considerable attention.

A fourth factor at play is a curious philosophy that has come to influence our everyday living. It is called postmodernism. We have watched this strange creed crawl out of the closets of academia and take up residence in our families and neighbourhoods. It is the child of a rather loose gathering of philosophers and social theorists who have criticized the basic ideas we have used to organize social and political life.[18] They have watched the rise of international violence and multiculturalism, and they recognize that violent conflict and cultural diversity are not new. What they argue for, however, is a new recognition of the limits of reason or rationality in dealing with the conflicts arising from diversity.

Our hope in past centuries was in reason. We believed rationality could rise above cultural and religious differences and unite us in the project of democracy. We thought that reason was shared by all, and we had figured out how it worked. What we have found in the intervening years, however, was not one reason, but many. Theories of reason multiplied like the fishes of the sea. More than this, we discovered that culture shapes the way reason itself works. When the reason of one culture meets the reason of another, it pronounces it unreasonable. The net effect is that postmodernism pronounces the project of democracy much more complicated than we had thought. When facing conflicts, we can no longer ask each other to 'be reasonable.' The result has been a furious proliferation of studies of conflict that invite us to think, not simply about fixing conflict, but about living it differently.

Still, the fact remains that we do manage to handle some of our conflicts fairly well. In fact, at times, they even help us grow. And this observation is at the root of a fifth factor that has shaped our new-found attention to conflict. Philosophers and social scientists have come to regard conflict not simply as negative, but also as a potential for positive personal and social change. Conflict is no longer universally regarded as a problem to be solved, an evil to be exorcised. It can be good for us. Who knew?

This positive attitude towards conflict has its roots in the nineteenth century, in the work of a group of philosophers who discovered how conflict can function as a force for significant historical change.[19] The real shift occurred, however, in the twentieth century when psychologists and sociologists began exploring the dynamics of change in personal and social life.[20] They observed that we do not grow towards maturity along smooth, even paths. Rather, our lives unfold in fits and starts. We experience times of calm and times of turbulence, and often the turbulence functions as a catalyst for growth. A principal feature of turbulence is conflict. We may not enjoy the experience, but we can benefit from it. We can even grow from it. We can learn new skills for dealing with conflict, new attitudes towards conflict, and new ways of facing those problems in life we might previously have avoided because of our fear of conflict. What followed was a flurry of research on conflict as a potential for personal and social growth.

The result of all this is that we are deeply interested in conflict. We pay close attention to it. We notice it and talk about it in ways we would never have done before. We fear it, but we are fascinated by it. In a way, we are even attracted to it. We know we need to learn about it because we know it is with us in ways we had not experienced before. This is our interest in this book. We want to examine what we have learned about conflict and what we can glean from studying the learning that occurs when conflicts are handled well.

In particular, our focus is on the curious shift that occurs when we move from conflict to resolution. Resolution takes many forms: reaching agreement, discovering new paths, greeting difference differently, agreeing to disagree, accepting a ruling – the list goes on. In each case, if it is real, the resolution leaves us with a different attitude towards the issue and towards each other. Before resolution, the conflict divides us and blocks our ability to deal with the issue. After, even when we agree merely to comply, we relate differently and agree to move forward. In some important way, this shift is a change in us.

We all know that some resolutions are not fair. Some are downright oppressive. Feminist research has examined the way that gender imbalance and patriarchy are often involved in what we have called 'resolution.' Their analyses have led us to rethink the standards we use when evaluating what counts as resolution, and many question whether we ought to continue speaking of 'resolution' at all. Still, they have not given up differentiating between healthy and destructive ways of working through conflicts. For many feminists, the focus has shifted to an attention to relationships and the role of 'difference' in conflicts. We encounter others as different and this encounter can transform us.[21] It is this interest in transformation that we explore in the following chapters.

We have spoken of this transformation as learning, and our selection of language here may seem rather odd. We tend to think of learning in terms of teaching and curricula. Even when we think of learning out-

side of classroom settings, we still tend to think about formal procedures of teaching and acquiring information. It is difficult to resist
being drawn to traditional images of history as remembering dates and
chemistry as memorizing formulae. Learning theorists, however, have
pointed out that these images are profoundly misleading.[22] Memorizing information is not fully learning; it is a tiny piece of a much larger
process that is often mistaken for the whole process. In fact, focusing
exclusively on remembering data can derail the process of understanding. Moreover, much of the learning of our lives takes place outside of
formal processes. Much of it does not involve teachers.

Full learning is experiential, and it involves understanding, reflection, and action. It is a process that involves multiple stages and feedback loops that bring us back time and again to our experiences with
new questions, new attitudes, and new patterns of engagement. As the
fuller process unfolds, researchers have observed that learners themselves are changed, not simply at the level of ideas, but also at the level
of feeling and caring. It is this kind of change that can be observed in
conflicts when they are handled well.

Transformation through Learning

There are many theories of learning and each has its own map of the
learning process and its own interest in particular learning contexts.[23]
One of the most compelling approaches for our purposes is the Transformative Learning Theory of Jack Mezirow. His focus is on adult
learners and the way learning changes the learner. Mezirow and his
associates have been studying the transformative process since the
1970s; their interest in adult learners began with Mezirow's study of a
group of women returning to college after having been out of school.[24]
He charted the process they experienced upon reentry, and noted how
their learning paths involved far more than simply acquiring the information of their programs.

What stood out for Mezirow was the way the women experienced
an initial period of disorientation, a sense of alienation and discontent
that challenged their sense of themselves and their world. He watched
them discover that they were not alone with these feelings and they
began sharing them with others. This seemed to open doors to exploring assumptions about themselves. A process of critical self-examina-
tion followed, and this ushered in a new phase of the learning process
that had an effect on their involvement in their respective programs of

study. They began exploring new possibilities for themselves, and along with this came a new-found self-confidence that eventually helped them reintegrate the knowledge and skills of their program into a new self-concept. Central to their learning, Mezirow discovered, was a transformation in their sense of themselves and the world in the learning process.

At the centre of Transformative Learning is the belief that, as adults, we have developed meaning perspectives that have the effect of colouring and filtering the way we interpret the events of our lives.[25] These meaning perspectives are ordered sets of ideas and expectations, and they frame our sense of ourselves and the world. As they develop, they become habitual and operate behind the scenes, hidden from our normal focus of attention. Most often, we do not even know about these perspectives, nor do we advert to the way they project assumptions and expectations onto our field of experiences. They organize our ideas, and they shape and filter the way we interpret others and ourselves in relation to them.

There are occasions when learning can assimilate new experiences and ideas into our meaning perspectives. Learning begins to change us most dramatically, however, when new experiences do not fit into existing perspectives and we begin to feel challenged in our sense of ourselves and our world. Mezirow turned to the work of philosopher Jürgen Habermas to help explain what goes on in this transformative process, and what he found was Habermas's analysis of the role of distortions, prejudices, and stereotypes in our meaning perspectives.

Our meaning perspectives organize our world, and provide us with safe, known frameworks in which to live out our lives. However, these perspectives are never complete, nor are they without their problems. As we go through life we also develop assumptions and attitudes that distort our ability to relate to experience. These distortions have the effect of blocking new experiences and closing us off from other people. They cut off new lines of thinking and questioning, and limit our ability to differentiate and integrate new ideas.[26] When new experiences challenge our meaning perspectives, our resistance to change is not simply the result of the comfort zone created by our frames of reference; it is also the result of distortions at work within them. At this point, we only move beyond the distortions by invoking a new attitude, a pattern of reflection – what Habermas calls an 'interest' – that turns us from reflecting on the outside world to reflecting critically upon ourselves. Habermas calls this the emancipatory interest.[27]

When we give full rein to the emancipatory interest, we enter into the process of critical self-reflection and this is the decisive stage in transformative learning. This is the phase that brings us most profoundly in touch with the hidden side of ourselves. Oddly enough, it is also the stage that brings us into the most vigorous interaction with others. This is because our learning, here, gets shaped by the process of communication. Our learning is informed, not simply by what we are thinking, but by how others challenge our thinking. We begin opening up to their challenges, and shift to a new critical attitude towards ourselves and our assumptions. Here we begin turning our reflection and questioning onto the hidden assumptions buried in our own meaning perspectives. The questioning of others invites us to examine distortions at work in us, blocking and deforming our interpretations. We begin exploring alternatives that open our horizons to new learning, and this opens new ways of relating to others and new ways of achieving consensus on issues that would otherwise divide us.[28]

Mezirow's theory is rich. He offers an analysis of the transformative process in learning and a well recognized philosophical framework for understanding how and why this process works. Still, what of the transformative moment itself? What is the difference between a response to a challenge that leaves us hardened in our original perspective and one that moves us to a new stage of self-reflection? What happens in these moments? Mezirow and his colleagues offer some help here. They offer analyses of 'learner empowerment.'[29] They explore 'trigger events' in terms of 'disorienting dilemmas.'[30] And their analysis, generally, focuses on the social conditions that can be created to usher learners through the transformative phases of the process. Yet they also leave us with further questions about the personal side of the process.

Influenced as it is by Habermas, Mezirow's focus is on transformative learning as a social process of communication. Throughout his own career, Habermas's preoccupation was with the social structure of communication and how an analysis of communication furnishes social norms for healthy discourse in democratic society. Mezirow's work reflects this social focus. His theory reflects the preoccupation with the social side of learning, and it does leave us with further questions about the personal side of the process. What goes on in these personal moments, and how are they related to the social dynamics of learning?

Interestingly enough, these questions have been asked of Habermas's own work, and not simply by his critics. In his book on the discourse ethics of Habermas, William Rehg draws attention to the personal experience of insight.[31] Insight is deeply personal, yet it is not merely personal. His analysis brings to light a curious relationship between the social and personal sides of communication.

> Do not the experiences of insight and conviction – of getting the point, of catching on to a solution, of hitting the target squarely with an answer – do not such experiences, after all, reside within the individual? A focus on the kind of problem solving employed in arriving at factual judgments, in scientific research, in mathematics, or even in solving crossword puzzles, encourages an affirmative answer to these questions. Nonetheless, even in such monologically inclined pursuits the presence of the intersubjective makes itself felt.[32]

Rehg goes on to explain how insights occur in social contexts and are evaluated within the social communicative process elaborated by Habermas. What he signals, however, is important for our purposes. The transformative moment in learning – the experience that shifts us from the status quo to a new learning moment – does have this deeply personal side. Our interest is in pursuing the further questions that explore this personal side. And, to do this, we take up the invitation extended by Rehg to turn our attention to the Insight Theory of Canadian philosopher, Bernard Lonergan.

Conflict and Learning: Contributions from Lonergan's Insight Theory

The Insight Theory of Lonergan provides resources for answering some of these questions about learning and conflict resolution. Lonergan's philosophy focuses on personal transformation: how it occurs, and how it functions both cognitively and affectively to shift meaning perspectives.[33] What Lonergan adds is a focus on the role of insight in the transformation process. Insights have a curious shape and texture to them, they come in different types, each with its own distinctive role in the learning process. They affect our cognition as well as our feeling and valuing. They are deeply personal experiences, yet they occur in social contexts and their import is profoundly social.

At the centre of Lonergan's philosophy is a method of focusing attention on our own acts of insight. It involves 'catching ourselves' as we seek to understand the ideas of others or as we puzzle through problems. This activity is personal in the sense that we must each do it for ourselves. But it is social since we can engage in conversations with others about our self-discoveries, and these conversations can reshape the way we attend to ourselves and our experiences and help verify our insights. What we discover is that learning is not a single action that can be explained either as a passive reception of information, or as an active construction of meanings, ideas, or systems. Rather, learning takes place through a sequence of operations, each of which involves both passive and active dimensions.

Insights are answers to questions, and they only begin to emerge when we give ourselves over to genuine wonder, interest, curiosity, and questioning. They require attention to our fields of experience and the way we use images to help capture and portray our experiences. This attention must be careful, it must attend to details, it must expect the unexpected. It often requires that we get up out of our chairs and immerse ourselves differently in life experiences. We may think we can understand mathematics reading a book, but this is not so when it comes to understanding children. In fact, understanding mathematics well requires making links to life experiences. To understand new things requires entering into new worlds of feeling, seeing, tasting, and relating. Insight is deeply experiential, and can only occur when the experiences begin to wash over us.

When insights do occur, they often come as a surprise. This is why catching ourselves in the act of insight is so difficult. Not only do they arise unexpectedly, but their effect is to transform our field of meaning. What previously was incomprehensible is now clearly obvious. Where previously we stood in the face of a jumbled mass of disparate fragments, now we grasp an ordered whole. In fact, this transformation in us is so total and complete that, before the insight, we cannot imagine it, and after, we have difficulty retrieving our prior state of confusion.

Insights begin with questioning, yet questions are never neutral; they focus our curiosity in certain directions, and for insights to occur, our questions need to be on the right track. We often experience this sort of thing in trying to understand others. We think they are saying one thing, and so our questions follow along this line, but then we discover that they are talking about something quite different. To understand their meaning requires shifting our line of questioning. Our questions must relate to the experiences, and this means that the road to insight requires careful attention to questions. Getting insights often requires shifting patterns of questioning, and these shifts involve a second type of insight – the inverse insight – that functions in a different sort of way.

Here we do not discover answers to questions; we discover that if we want to make sense of some experience or understand another person, we are on the wrong line of questioning. In the chapters that follow, we explore some interesting ways that inverse insights operate in conflicts to help us along transformative paths of learning.

While insights mark a dramatic shift in our field of meaning, they are not the end of the learning process. For insights to become knowledge, they must be verified. Verification requires that we return to our field of experience and ask a set of questions about the links among the insight, the question, and the data of experience. Have we faced all the relevant questions? Does the insight answer all our questions? Does it meet the questions head on, or does it supply a piece of a bigger puzzle? What about the bigger puzzle? These subsequent steps bring us back into the circles or loops of experiencing, puzzling, shifting lines of questioning, getting insights, sharing with others, verifying, and putting ideas into action. As we move through the circles of operations, we are brought back, again and again, through the learning process that subtly but powerfully shapes and reshapes us as persons.

One of the most dramatic aspects of Lonergan's work is his understanding of feelings and the way they carry values that orient us towards people and events. Feelings do their work by guiding our attention, our lines of interest, our responses to others, and the direction of our actions. But the values that lie behind the feelings are often not known to us. They have been formed experientially, but may not have been subjected to our explicit work of understanding and decision. We are familiar with the texture of the feeling, but we have not understood what it is about. The result is that feelings play a dramatic role in guiding our relations with others in conflicts. Until we engage explicitly in understanding these feelings and the cares and threats that lie behind them, we will not know what is driving our conflicts. Getting insights into feelings, cares, and threats can play a powerful role in helping us work through conflicts. This often involves appreciating what is valued by others and probing what lies behind our own feelings of threat.

As we move through the Insight Theory of Lonergan, we are introduced to the method of self-discovery, we assemble a group of different kinds of insights, and we explore the role of feelings and values in shaping our interactions with others in situations of conflict. We come to discern an overall pattern or structure in the way these operations work together to yield learning, and we explore how Insight Theory can complement and enhance the Transformative Learning approach to learning. We explore how this learning can help us in wrestling with the conflicts that are so much a part of our relations with others. We explore how insight sheds light on many of the assumptions about conflict we carry with us in our involvement in personal and public life. This is our itinerary in the following chapters.

Now that the Stage Is Set

Our goal in this chapter has been to introduce a line of inquiry: a line of thinking about conflict and conflict resolution. Conflict is an ordinary part of everyday life. Yet it is not often that we examine our assumptions about conflict and its implications for our involvement in social life. Democracy means diversity, and it means participation in our institutions of public life. Assuring this diversity and participation requires dealing with the conflicts that arise in our personal and public lives. But how are we to do this? Do we expect conflicts to be handled by professionals, or are we becoming more involved personally? Are our institutions requiring more citizen participation? If so, what does this require of us as citizens?

We began with a series of snapshots that illustrate different ways of thinking about conflict resolution, criminal justice, and democracy. In each snapshot, we observe a more traditional and an alternative approach. In the traditional approaches, experts or professionals do the work of resolving conflicts, securing justice on behalf of citizens when conflicts become crimes, and establishing the conditions for democratic life. Citizens are involved, but not as principal actors. In the alternative approaches, citizen participation is more pronounced and more central to the business of public life. Democracy here is not something secured by professionals, but something that requires our ongoing involvement as citizens, and this means involvement in the work of resolving conflicts.

We are witnessing a call for greater citizen participation in public life. This does not mean abandoning traditional ideas and institutions, but it does mean a proliferation of alternative initiatives and new forms of involvement in the traditional institutions. Citizens are reluctant to leave justice and democracy to the professionals. Increasingly they have something to say in public life, and this is shaping citizen involvement in both traditional institutions and newly emerging initiatives.

Our interest is in exploring the implications of this citizen participation for our involvement in conflicts. Greater citizen involvement means greater participation in resolving conflicts, and this means understanding what this requires of us. Whether we go through the courts or use more informal processes, resolving conflicts leaves us transformed in subtle but important ways. Resolution may involve wholehearted agreement, or it may be mere compliance. In both cases something important happens to shift us from a state of conflict to resolution. We suggest this transformation involves learning, and our interest is in exploring what is involved in this learning. It might seem odd to call this learning. Yet learning research supports this line of inquiry. Understanding the transformations involved in this learning is essential for enhancing our involvement in the conflict resolution that is at the heart of our personal and public lives. Our focus, then, is on the role that Lonergan's Insight Theory can play in understanding the transformative learning involved in the conflicts of democratic life.

2 Studying Conflict: Where Have We Arrived and Why Think About Insight?

In 1987, Kenneth Boulding was invited to write the foreword to a volume of essays on conflict edited from a series of lectures delivered at George Mason University between 1981 and 1982.[1] The lectures were held in conjunction with the launching of the University's new Center for Conflict Resolution and its new Master of Science program in Conflict Management. During these years, universities, governments, and other organizations across North America and Europe were scrambling to launch research institutes and programs of study on conflict. Boulding wanted to situate this activity within the social and political context of the times and highlight the urgency of this work.

He begins with an anecdote illustrating his view of the predicament of the human race. He compares the world to a tribe living atop a mesa surrounded by cliffs. The tribe is divided into two factions, each led by a leader who is single-mindedly dedicated to winning a race run against the other. The tribes are committed to following their leaders in the race, and all roads lead to edges of the cliff. Unless the leaders and their followers can be persuaded to stop and think about their predicament, the outcome can only be disaster for all. Boulding introduces the book of essays as an important contribution to this process of stopping and reflecting on the human predicament.

Boulding's anecdote captures something of the atmosphere of the times. On the political front, tensions between East and West were fuelling a dangerous nuclear arms race that threatened the future of the planet. On the environmental front, growing public awareness of the limits to the planet's carrying capacity heightened concerns over potentially disastrous patterns of economic growth.[2] On the domestic front, the courts were being taxed beyond their capacities, and reports of family abuse and community violence filled the newspapers. At the centre of all of these problems lie human conflicts, and in the air was a growing conviction that we can no longer handle conflicts as we have done in the past.[3]

This period of the 1970s and 1980s marked a dramatic moment in the study of conflict. Scholars see in these years the emergence of conflict as a distinct field of scholarly study and a distinct field of professional practice. Theorists and practitioners from such fields as law, psychology, management, politics, sociology, international relations, ethics, religion, philosophy, and family studies were now asking how their research might be brought together to provide resources for dealing with some of the troublesome problems threatening human societies. To be sure, studying conflict did not begin in the 1970s. What did emerge, however, was a growing awareness that common lines of analysis could be discerned in the diverse fields of human experience and this could make a difference for human societies. Scholars began to see themselves as working together to advance a common fund of knowledge on conflict that could enhance our ability to live together on the planet.

What is important about this period is not only the convergence of disciplines but the convergence of theory and practice. Theorists and researchers who, to this point, had confined their work to university libraries and laboratories, now began meeting with negotiators, mediators, lawyers, and judges. What emerged was a conviction that this fund of scholarly knowledge could both inform and be informed by the experiences gained from practice. People wrestling with conflicts in real life could learn from this growing body of research, but they also had something to say to the scholars. A disciplined reflection on their experiences could shift the direction of research and generate new lines of theory. The hope was that this interdisciplinary learning on conflict could benefit from the exchange between theorists and practitioners, and the results of this exchange could enhance our ability to manage the conflicts of our lives more effectively and responsibly.

One of the themes signalled by Boulding and pervasive throughout the literature of this period was the idea that conflict research was now to be informed by 'scholarly knowledge' rather than simply 'folk knowledge.'[4] Decades later, we are inclined to greet this distinction with caution. We have witnessed too many disasters created by so-called scientific approaches to human problems, and we have come to appreciate the considerable wisdom to be found in the traditional practices of diverse cultures. Still, Boulding's point was that managing conflict is complex and difficult. It requires careful study and the development of skills. Scholarly knowledge must build upon folk knowledge. We need to study this complexity and verify which skills do indeed lead to more humane responses to conflict. This is the task of scholarship. Boulding was convinced that far too many of the world's conflicts were being handled by leaders with inadequate tools and skills. His call was for scholars to provide them with better resources for handling the complexities they faced in the field. The result was the development of conflict research.

Conflict as a Positive Experience

Readers who browse through the literature from these years are struck by a curious ambivalence in attitudes towards conflict. On the one hand, the discussions of many of the studies evoke feelings of pain and suffering. Conflict must be resolved because it is traumatic: people get hurt, and families, communities, and nations get ripped apart. Conflict is associated with dysfunctional workplaces and nasty child custody battles where children come out the victims. Ultimately, it is associated with war, and in the age of nuclear weapons, war means the annihilation of humanity. We are left with the feeling that conflict does indeed plague our lives.

What is striking, however, is another attitude that emerges in the literature: conflict can be a positive growth experience. What an idea! In his overview of the 'organizational conflict' papers from a 1987 conference, Dean Tjosvold makes the bold statement that managers and employees can learn skills that can make conflict a productive part of organizational life. Traditional management theorists like Frederick Taylor assumed that conflict disrupted organizations. They sought efficiency, rationality, and smooth-functioning order. Conflict must be ended decisively by management. Contemporary theorists, however, view organizations differently. They seek the commitment and involvement of employees, not merely their compliance. Healthy organizations require open discussion and participation, and this means that conflict will always be a part of organizational life. Learning the attitudes, tools, and skills for managing conflict can help make it a productive part of organizational life. Conflict can be good for organizations.[5]

This view that conflict can be a positive experience became an integral part of the research of the 1970s and 1980s. It was not a new idea, however. It was developed in the 1950s by sociologist Lewis Coser,[6] as an effort to challenge some of the prevailing currents in social theory of the time, and it has its roots in the work of the nineteenth-century German philosophers Hegel and Marx.

Coser's work, *The Functions of Social Conflict*, was published in 1956, and his interest was in the processes of social change. At the time, prominent American social theorists like Talcott Parsons and Robert Merton were interested in the stability of social structures. They were fascinated with how social processes emerge and take on a life of their own without being deliberately engineered or designed by individual people. Their questions were about structures, roles, and institutions whose form and function precede individuals, remain stable, and live on after their death. Their theories sought to explain things like social coherence and the recurrence of similar patterns of social organization in diverse times and places. They were interested in conflict, but their questions tended to ask about stability and how social structures survive the disruptive effects of conflicts.[7]

Coser's questions were different. He wanted to know how social structures change. More than this, he wanted to know how they live on through continual change and how conflict plays a positive role in this ongoing dynamic of change. Views of conflict that had dominated social theory since Plato tended to see conflict only as disruptive. To survive, societies needed strong guardians who would quell conflict and maintain harmony. Coser's ideas of social health, however, were broader in scope. He focused on the more oppressive forms of social order that can arise in societies and the way conflict can break the grip of these forces. He examined how conflict can form and strengthen social groups. He studied how conflict can maintain checks and balances against the totalitarian tendencies that arise from a centralization of power. For Coser, the very idea of social health was centred around an equilibrium maintained by conflict itself.

He acknowledged his debt to the nineteenth-century German philosophers Hegel and Marx, who developed theories that recognized the role of conflict in the processes of society and history.[8] What Hegel and Marx discovered was the idea that social change does not move along smooth, harmonious paths. It involves conflict, upheaval, turbulence. Moreover, this upheaval is not to be understood only as a destructive force. Quite the contrary. The negative forces of society and history are permanent features of the very structure of society and, indeed, of human consciousness itself. Negation and conflict are at the source of their vitality. This is because social order is not simply about harmony, it is also about oppression, and social vitality means wrestling with oppression.

The key to this analysis is the way that conflict arises from a negative experience, but becomes a positive force for overturning this negative experience. Conflict, here, becomes a force that helps liberate social groups from the grip of domination. This gives it a positive role in the longer-term process of social change. Karl Marx developed his own theory with a focus on violent revolution. Subsequent social theorists like Jürgen Habermas, however, learned from the bitter experiences of Soviet domination, and they began examining more peaceful ways that conflict can function to promote democracy.[9] The other feature of the analysis was the idea of human freedom. Marx's theory tended to see the social-historical process as mechanical or deterministic, operating regardless of human freedom and responsibility. Subsequent theorists understood the process differently, as including and requiring human acts of freedom. Conflict presents opportunities that can be harnessed to shift social groups from dysfunctional to more healthy patterns of relations. Responding to the opportunities presented by conflict becomes one of the integral features of human communication, and handling it responsibly becomes an essential part of democracy.[10]

It was this idea of conflict as a potential for positive social change that interested researchers in the field. They were not Marxists. Neither were they interested in promoting violent revolution as an instrument of social change. What they did pursue was the idea that conflict generated forces and opportunities which, if harnessed well, could promote personal and social growth. One of the most outspoken proponents of this positive idea of conflict was Morton Deutsch, and he introduced one of his lectures at George Mason University with an anecdote that captured the feelings of the time.

A British political scientist, John Burton (1972),[11] has said that conflict is like sex. It is an important and pervasive aspect of life. It should be enjoyed and should occur with a reasonable degree of frequency. After conflict is over, people should feel better as a result ...

It prevents stagnation, it stimulates interest and curiosity. It is the medium through which problems can be aired and solutions arrived at. It is the root of personal and social changes. And conflict is often part of the process of testing and assessing oneself. As such it may be highly enjoyable as one experiences the pleasure of the full and active use of one's capacities. In addition, conflicts demarcate groups from one another and help establish group and personal identities.[12]

When applied to the study of organizations, Deutsch's ideas had powerful implications. He outlined the difference between cooperative and competitive approaches to conflict and traced their implications for organizational life. Competitive approaches view conflict in terms of winners and losers. Parties see their own interests as requiring them to challenge or overcome the other. To achieve their goals they must argue their position strongly, hold fast to their stance, defend their arguments, and find flaws in the other's. Their focus is not on the strength of the other's position but on the weaknesses. The aim is winning, and this means accepting whatever costs must be paid. Frequently, the result of competitive exchanges is hurt feelings, damaged relationships, and the feeling that future problems cannot be solved without the imposition of authority or force.[13]

Cooperative approaches view conflict quite differently. Here parties pursue their goals with the assumption that their achievement is linked to the achievement of the other's goals. Their interest is in win-win outcomes, and problems are viewed as mutual. When confronted with opposition, they feel challenge and resistance, but they greet this challenge with curiosity. Their assumption is that understanding the merits in the other's argument and the shortcomings in their own can help better achieve their mutual goals. The result of cooperative exchanges is often good will and the feeling that future problems can be resolved together.[14]

Organizational theorists picked up on this line of analysis and explored its application to the field of management. Organizations are systems of interdependent actors. They have goals and interests that both converge and conflict. But because they are interdependent, dealing constructively with their conflicts can be a route for achieving the shared goals and interests of the organization. Their conclusion was that conflict is not necessarily a symptom of an organization's dysfunction; it can be a normal part of its healthy functioning. More than this, conflict can present organizations with opportunities for learning and development. Researchers studied the effects of cooperative and competitive approaches on organizational development. They concluded that cooperative approaches generally foster a better climate for organizational development. They also explored the conditions under which competitive approaches could be useful.[15] The overall result was a shift in attitude towards organizational conflict. Conflict can, indeed, play a positive role in enhancing cooperative relations in organizations.

Cooperation and Conflict: Game Theory

One of the early and prominent lines of scholarship influencing conflict studies was Game Theory. In 1944 John von Neumann and Oskar Morgenstern published their influential *Theory of Games and Economic Behavior*, and their work gave rise to a tremendous proliferation of mathematical and computerized laboratory research on conflict. This research challenged many existing assumptions about competitive approaches to conflict, and it was interpreted as offering a truly scientific basis for approaching conflicts cooperatively.[16]

Game theory sets up simple experimental models in which two or more persons are given scenarios in which they must achieve specified objectives in situations where they interact with others in defined ways. One of the examples provided by Morton Deutsch was a game in which two trucking firms, Acme and Bolt, must pass over a one-lane stretch of road in opposing directions in order to reach their respective destinations.[17] The players must negotiate with each other on how to get their trucks through the one-lane bottleneck. To get paid, they must deliver their merchandise to their destinations, and the amount they are paid is determined, in part, by the amount of time it takes them to make the delivery. Winners are determined by amounts of money earned in a defined set of trials of the game. The paths available to the players are set by the researchers, and players can develop either competitive or cooperative ways of negotiating their way to their destination.

The key to Game Theory is that one party cannot achieve her goal without negotiating a conflict with the other. By allowing participants a succession of trials of the game to try out various strategies for attaining objectives, researchers observe and document the tendencies of participants to choose either competitive or cooperative strategies. More than this, however, they observe how the players learn from their experiences and from their opponents' reactions in a succession of trials. They compile statistics on whether competitive or cooperative strategies cumulatively yield better or worse outcomes for players, and they formulate both descriptive and normative conclusions regarding competitive or cooperative approaches to conflict. The most compelling conclusion of Game Theory research was that cooperative strategies are more conducive to attaining one's own goals. This attracted considerable attention.

The Game Theory research that most influenced conflict studies involved a type of scenario called 'the prisoners dilemma.' The scenario involves two prisoners who have been partners in committing a crime and who have been captured and are held in separate prison cells with no chance of speaking with each other.[18] The evidence proves that they have committed a minor crime with a prison sentence of one year. However the prosecuting attorney knows but cannot prove that they have also committed a major crime with a sentence of nine years. Both are asked to either confess or deny committing the major crime, and the assigned outcomes involve four possibilities: (1) if they both confess, they both get a sentence of nine years for the major crime but nothing for the minor crime; (2) if A confesses and B denies, A gets off free as a witness in the trial but B earns jail terms for both crimes, a total of ten years; (3) if B confesses and A denies, B gets off free, and A earns a ten-year jail term; (4) if both deny, they both get only one-year jail terms for the minor crime. Because they are held in separate cells with no chance of communicating with each other, both must decide what to do on the basis of assumptions about what the other will do.

The scenario has been modified in its description in many different ways to illustrate a wide range of human situations, some involving avoiding negative consequences and others involving attaining positive objectives for themselves and others. Researchers set up a succession of iterations of the game in which players try a strategy, observe the behaviour of the other player, tabulate their results, then try a succession of following strategies in the hope of maximizing their outcomes. The basic idea of the game circles around the difference between self-interested approaches and cooperative approaches to conflict. If players regard their options in a purely self-interested way, they observe that they can most safely avoid the worst results for themselves (ten years in jail), and possibly achieve the best results (no jail time) by confessing. The most risky strategy for each is denying because this leaves each of them most vulnerable if the other confesses. But denial is also the most cooperative strategy, since it is the way optimal outcomes are achieved by both (only one year in jail for each of them).

Game Theory research brings to light many of the assumptions and expectations that we carry with us in our experiences of conflict. In particular, it highlights the role played by our expectations of others. If we expect others to be self-interested and non-cooperative, we may wish to be cooperative, but we often conclude that our own cooperative behaviour only leaves us vulnerable to being exploited by them. What also emerges, however, is the way that a succession of trials can provide an environment for communication, learning, and trust-building between players. One of the most celebrated books of this period was a volume by Robert Axelrod, *The Evolution of Cooperation*, which focused on the results of a researcher at the University of Toronto, Anatol Rapoport. What Rapoport discovered was that by modelling and rewarding cooperative behaviour and strategically penalizing the adversary's non-cooperative behaviour, players could get opponents to cooperate, with the result that they consistently achieved the best outcomes for themselves.

Axelrod was fascinated by Rapoport's conclusions. They seemed to imply that, under certain conditions, cooperation could emerge even among self-interested parties. He asked whether this learning process towards cooperation might have much wider implications for social and evolutionary theory than previously thought. Instead of thinking of biological and social evolution entirely in terms of competition for survival, he argued that the most robust strategies for survival are indeed cooperative rather than competitive.

The influence of Game Theory on the study of conflict was enormous, and one of the dramatic areas in which its influence was felt was in the theatre of international negotiations. In hindsight, we look back on the 1980s as the period approaching the end of the Soviet Union and the Cold War era. During these years, however, the shape of future events had not yet become clear, and representatives from both East and West were putting their heads together to develop new ways for handling the growing conflicts arising in what came to be regarded as an 'emerging system of international negotiation.'[19]

In 1972, representatives from the United States and the U.S.S.R. joined forces to launch the International Institute for Applied Systems Analysis (IIASA). The organization was dedicated to scientific exchanges among representatives from countries of the East and West, and its goal was to explore how scientific collaboration might help promote a climate of international cooperation.[20] One of the projects of the Institute was a study of the Processes of International Negotiation (PIN), and in 1991 a 486-page volume of essays from the project was published documenting the results of six years of research and consultation. In his overview essay, Victor Kremenyuk points to Game Theory and the work of Axelrod as offering a scientific basis for a major shift in international negotiations: a shift away from self-interested bargaining and towards a 'joint problem-solving approach.'[21] He points to a series of treaties where the joint problem-solving approach was used successfully as a basis for negotiations. And he offers a range of recommendations on how more and more of the world's international conflicts could be handled in an environment of 'nonviolence, joint problem solving, cooperation, and common values and language.'[22]

The Experience of Conflict Practitioners: Interest Theory

Game Theory influenced conflict studies considerably. But on its own, it was judged insufficient. Conflict research needed the contributions of practitioners working in the field, and the result was the development of Interest Theory, a practice-based approach whose impact would be felt in decades to come.

Harvard University professor Howard Raiffa illustrates this shift in attention from computer models to the field of practice. As advisor to McGeorge Bundy for four years, Raiffa experienced first-hand many of the challenges of negotiating conflicts in complex international settings. Originally trained as a mathematical Game Theorist, Raiffa first expected the computer models to provide strategies that could be implemented in practice. What he found, however, was that they were not enough. Real-life negotiations called for a range of skills and analytic tools that were not captured in the sophisticated computer models. The 'science' of the computer laboratories might provide a foundation for basic ideas and attitudes, but real-life negotiating was also an 'art.' It required a wide range of flexible lines of analysis that could be adapted to diverse situations. And it required skills that could only be developed through considerable experience and practice.[23]

While Game Theorists were busy with their laboratories, theories, and computer models, a host of negotiators, mediators, lawyers, and arbitrators were at work wrestling with real-life conflicts in every field of personal and social life. Their work focused not on theoretical elegance but on practical applications, and their interest was in the development of tools and skills that could improve participants' abilities to work through difficult conflicts. A key observation of the practitioners was that frequently the forces driving and sustaining conflicts are not the issues that focus the attention of parties and define their positions. Instead, resolving conflicts requires exploring deeper 'interests' that lie behind the positions. This distinction between 'positions' and 'interests' was the central feature of Interest Theory, and it became a guiding principle for conflict practitioners that would prove extremely durable.

One of the popular Interest Theory texts was a small book written by the director and associate director of the Harvard Negotiation Project, William Ury and Roger Fisher. The book was entitled *Getting to Yes: Negotiating Agreement Without Giving In.* Heralded by John Kenneth Galbraith as 'by far the best thing I've ever read about negotiation,'[24] the book is deceptively simple. While presented for a popular audience, it summarizes the achievements of a considerable body of practical experience and reflects the results of a wide range of research studying and evaluating the fruits of this experience. The authors provide four simple guidelines for enhancing the practice of negotiation:

- Separate the PEOPLE from the problem.
- Focus on INTERESTS, not positions.
- Invent OPTIONS for Mutual Gain.
- Insist on Using Objective CRITERIA.[25]

At the core of Interest Theory is the second guideline, 'Focus on INTERESTS, not positions.' Our standard approach to conflict is to focus on the issues under dispute. This is where we take our stand and establish our demands, or in conflict resolution language, claim our positions. It is standard because it is natural and habitual. It is what we have done throughout our lives, and this past experience shapes our spontaneous response to future conflicts. But the authors point out that there are two types of issues in a conflict, positions and interests.[26] The interests are the deeper concerns and needs underlying the positions. In most conflicts, what ground and sustain the dispute are not the explicit issues that focus our attention, but the underlying interests: the concerns, values, fears, and human needs that often go unnamed and unacknowledged.

It is important that underlying interests be identified, and they must be discussed and dealt with openly if conflicts are to be resolved.[27] Frequently, however, disputants do not discuss their interests because they have difficulty articulating them: they may have never formulated them, and they do not understand how they are at work in themselves and the other party. More than this, often they do not know how to discover them. Negotiators and mediators need to probe for the underlying feelings and concerns that reveal the deeper interests.[28] This can be difficult. Furthermore, disputants need to recognize the other's interests. This too can be difficult, particularly when the other's interests seem to pose a threat to their own.[29]

The authors present these ideas in an upbeat style with examples that illustrate what seem to be simple solutions to age-old problems. But the careful reader does not miss the challenge presented by their diagnoses and prescriptions. It is the challenge posed by habits and reflexes accumulated through the tumultuous experiences of life. Conflict practitioners know that common-sense ideas and skills are usually the least common things to be found in the midst of heated disputes. Interest Theory helped probe the complexity of conflicts and the skills required to negotiate this complexity. Studying the contexts of conflicts and the environments appropriate for this practice-based skill development became one of the important lines of practitioner research and reflection.

The Intractability of Conflict: Human Needs Theory

In contrast to the upbeat tone of Interest Theory, Human Needs Theory addressed the darker side of conflict. Developed by John Burton, a former Australian diplomat influential in establishing the academic study of conflict in Britain and the United States,[30] Human Needs Theory proposed that conflict is motivated by forces more basic than individual interests. It results from universal, non-negotiable needs that are not being met in existing situations. Burton argued that conflict is an indicator that all is not right in society. He was critical of approaches that focused on resolution and social harmony within the context of existing norms and institutions. Burton's claim was that if basic human needs remain unmet, measures aimed at social harmony would not succeed. Consequently, he proposed a generic theory of conflict with tools for diagnosing basic needs at work in all types of conflicts.

For Burton, human needs are basic requirements necessary for all persons to lead fully human lives. The idea of basic human needs originally had been developed by psychologist Abraham Maslow in the 1950s.[31] But while Maslow proposed a hierarchical ordering of needs, Burton's approach rejected this hierarchy and drew on British sociologist Paul Sites[32] to ground human needs in the sociobiology of E.O. Wilson.

Burton lists eight basic needs: consistency, stimulation, security, recognition, distributive justice, rationality before others, meaning, and a sense of control over one's actions.[33] All must be fulfilled for persons to develop and live fully, and if any are thwarted by dysfunctional social arrangements, conflict can be expected. To help explain why individuals resort to extreme measures to satisfy needs, Burton argued for a ninth need: 'role defence.' He was interested in how minority groups engaged in violence to attain goals that otherwise seemed irrational, and how those in power remained unwilling to accommodate the needs of minorities. In his view, both violent rebellion and repressive treatment of minorities resulted from people's unexpressed or unacknowledged need to fight to attain or retain a social role in which their other needs were satisfied. The ninth need had the effect of raising the stakes associated with the other eight.

What is important about Burton's Needs Theory is that he understands needs as socio-biologically preprogrammed: people *will* seek to satisfy unmet needs or protect those they feel are threatened. They will use any means at their disposal, and will pursue their basic needs even if they are not aware they are doing so. Most importantly, it explains why they will do so even if it causes them extreme suffering. Thus, Burton felt his theory of needs could explain the intractability of identity conflicts erupting around the world in the post-Second World War era. As long as the full range of security, recognition, justice, meaning, and control needs of minority groups are unmet, such conflicts remain inevitable. If this could be proven to be the case, then attempts to settle such conflicts via negotiations focused on interests would bring intrinsically unstable agreements.

Burton's theory of basic human needs remains one of the dominant theories in the field. Over the years, Burton has worked with others to design conflict resolution processes to help parties analyse their own and each other's underlying needs. His work has influenced the development of problem-solving workshops where parties in conflict come together in safe environments under the direction of skilled facilitators to explore basic needs at stake in conflicts. These workshops have been influential in the conflict resolution field from the 1970s onward, and practitioner-theorists like Herbert Kelman, Christopher Mitchell, Michael Banks, and Ronald Fisher have written extensively on their application to local and international contexts.[34]

The Complexity of Conflict: Communication Theory

Since the 1970s and 1980s, world events have given rise to significant changes in the study of conflict, and some of the most dramatic of these have come from the international arena. The changes in international relations since the end of the Soviet Union have shifted our focus from the East-West nuclear conflict of the superpowers to the diverse conflicts arising in such places as the former Yugoslavia, Somalia, Rwanda, Iraq, Haiti, Afghanistan, and Sudan. The experience of the 11 September 2001 attacks on the World Trade Center and the Pentagon in the United States and the wars in Iraq and Afghanistan have brought the spectre of violent conflict much closer to home for North Americans. Studies have broadened and deepened our understanding of the role of culture, religion, and gender in conflicts. With growing attention to climate change, researchers continue to examine the roles of theory, practice, and advocacy in the field of environmental conflicts. And in all fields, researchers and practitioners continue to work together to develop models of intervention, institutional frameworks, and tools for evaluation research.

A common theme emerging in all of these areas of research has been the appreciation of the complexity introduced by identity and diversity, and leading the way in probing this complexity has been Communication Theory. What Communication Theorists discovered is that conflicts are not simply the result of interactions between parties with defined interests. Rather, they are more complex processes in which the very interests and identities of parties are shaped by the communication unfolding within conflicts. In communication, words, symbols, gestures, and actions shape who we are and our notions of what is real. This process is interactive, it is interpersonal, it is cultural, and it is dynamic. Conflicts are about meaning, and understanding the dynamics of meaning takes us into the analysis of how we are constituted by meaning in the processes of communication.[35]

Traditionally we viewed communication instrumentally, as a means for exchanging information. Our assumption was that we work out our meanings by ourselves, and when we want to share them with others, we draw on tools of communication.[36] Early in the twentieth century, however, social theorists like George Herbert Mead discovered that this traditional view does not capture what actually goes on in our interactions with others.[37] Mead observed that communication involves a curious process called 'role-taking.' In conversation, I both speak to you, and listen to you respond to what I have said. When I listen to your response, frequently something interesting arises in me that begins to shape both my own meanings and my sense of myself. Your response to me often reveals an interpretation of me that is quite different from my own image of myself. I begin 'seeing' myself, not just from my own perspective, but from yours. I begin taking the role of you, and in so doing I take on something of your meaning of me. Your interpretation of me has the effect of shaping my own sense of myself. This process is going on all the time, and it explains how our identities are shaped by society and culture. Needless to say, this process is never complete. But it does launch me in a direction in which my own meanings and identity are shaped socially within the process of communication itself.

Conflict theorists picked up on these discoveries, and began applying them to the study of conflict. They began examining conflicts, not simply as the result of predefined interests or needs, but as communication processes that reshape the interests, needs, and identities of parties. Interests and needs are not simply mine, they are developed in relation to you and my interpretations of you. They are developed in relation to how I think you are interpreting me. They are even shaped by things from my own past that affect my interpretation of you and my thoughts about your attitude towards me. All of this goes on within the conflict. The result is a more complex analysis of the dynamics of conflict. Personal identities and meanings come to be understood as intimately connected to the social relations arising within conflicts themselves.

The effect of Communication Theory was to give rise to a new perspective on conflict. Resolving conflicts need not be considered simply a matter of solving problems so we can get on with our lives. It is now central to the very living itself.[38] It was the link between communication and identity formation that caught the attention of conflict theorists. If identities and interests are themselves shaped within the dysfunctional communication patterns of conflict, then developing more constructive patterns of communication could have a positive effect on the formation of identity and interest. This could play a positive role in reshaping the dynamics of social and political life. Communication Theorists came to regard the analysis and resolution of conflict as an integral part of living and learning how to live in an increasingly multicultural world.

Responding to Conflict: The Growing Use of Mediation

Conflicts are difficult, and they often prove too difficult for participants to manage on their own. Even when we are armed with good negotiation skills, disputes often get the better of us. When this happens, it can make good sense to turn to a third party – not an adjudicator or arbitrator who will impose a solution, but a mediator, someone who will help us solve the conflict and leave the decision-making to us. An important and durable initiative for responding to conflict in a host of legal, social, and cultural disputes was mediation.

An old and common form of conflict resolution, mediation has roots in Jewish and Christian traditions, ancient Chinese and Japanese laws and customs, and traditional African and North American native practices. It emerged in the contemporary North American context as an efficient, flexible alternative to the adjudication processes of the justice system.[39] Mediation programs were developed in the 1960s and 1970s to focus on victim-offender reconciliation, alternative sentencing for young offenders, and family and community conflicts. They were originally championed by community groups and social justice advocates as measures for promoting greater community participation in achieving justice and social transformation. Since then, mediation has been embraced as an effective conflict resolution process in business, labour, government, international relations, the environment, workplaces, neighbourhoods, schools, churches, and interpersonal relations.[40]

In one of the most prominent of the early books in the field, *The Mediation Process*, Christopher Moore describes mediation as 'the intervention into a dispute or negotiation by an acceptable, impartial, and neutral third party who has no authoritative decision-making power to assist disputing parties in voluntarily reaching their own mutually acceptable settlement of issues in dispute.'[41] Key to this definition are the terms 'acceptable,' 'impartial,' and 'assist.' Unlike adjudication and arbitration, mediation involves third parties in the work of assisting disputants themselves in arriving at resolutions they find mutually acceptable. Mediators hold no stakes in the content of the dispute. Rather, they help disputants by managing the process. Their work is to open doors of communication and help parties recognize the legitimacy of the other party's involvement in the process. They facilitate the process, expand resources, and help explore problems. They can be 'agents of reality' to help construct realistic settlement frameworks. They can help educate participants in the skills of communication, and they can take some of the heat off disputants who are charged with the task of negotiating on behalf of others. They can exercise leadership in moving negotiations forward with procedural and, at times, even substantive suggestions.[42] Flexibility and creativity are central features of mediation.

Researchers outline the stages involved in the mediation process. Different models describe the stages differently, but most outline a series of steps that parties need to work through if they are to achieve successful outcomes. The first stages are those that precede the actual mediation session itself. These are the initial contact stages where mediators meet the parties, get their commitment to the process, select a mediation strategy, gather background information, and design the mediation plan. The principal work here is to prepare the participants for the process and prepare the process for the participants. Mediation can only work if parties give their full consent to the process, and this can involve considerable preparatory work building a climate for trust and cooperation.

Next comes the mediation itself. It opens with an outline of the process, guidelines or protocols for participants, and the parties' initial statements about the issues and topics of concern. Then the mediator goes to work. Mediators know that conflicts involve relationships that can have long histories and deeper interests that undergird parties' positions in conflicts. Through questioning and probing, they help participants move beyond their initial positions to identify the interests underlying the dispute. Usually these are not known to the other party, and often they are not known even to parties themselves. Uncovering and identifying these hidden interests sets the grounds for the next stage where parties generate and assess options for settlement that will meet their interests. Finally, agreements are bargained, decided, and formulated, and strategies are devised for implementing the results of the agreement. Informal agreements or formal documents are drafted and signed, and the mediation process concludes.[43]

Mediation is available as an alternative conflict resolution process and as a fully integrated component within traditional justice institutions. In either context, participant satisfaction levels are high, not simply because of outcomes, but also because of the sense of participation and control parties feel in shaping the direction of the process.[44] In mediations, parties can judge what will meet their interests, they can engage creatively in the decision-making process, they can explore integrative, win-win outcomes, and they can emerge feeling like authors of their own solutions.[45] Through the decades, statistics on user satisfaction tend to be good, rates of compliance tend to be favourable, and data on efficiency and speed of settlement have been good. Most important, however, have been the effects on the post-dispute climate. Mediations seem to get more effectively to the heart of the matter, to the relationship issues in the dispute. The result has been more durable settlements.[46] There can be no doubt that conflicts remain difficult challenges for participants, but experienced mediators can help parties take a more active and constructive role in the resolution process, and this can play an important role in achieving effective and durable outcomes.

Mediators have become a permanent part of our lives in business, in the justice system, in neighbourhoods, in the education system, in personal relationships, and in politics. Traditional dispute resolution mechanisms that in the past relied heavily on adjudicators and arbitrators, now make room for mediators, and mediation is part of the mandated practices in many of the institutions of social life. Researchers now regard negotiation and mediation processes as a continuum, involving similar sets of tools and skills. Participants in conflicts can learn the tools and use them to negotiate their own way through conflicts. But when the challenges prove too daunting, they can call in mediators who will use them on their behalf. Mediators help participants achieve what they cannot achieve on their own.

Models of Mediation: Interest-Based, Transformative, and Narrative

What has developed in the field of mediation is a diversity of models, each offering its own approach to conflict and conflict resolution.[47] Mediators now situate themselves in relation to one or another of the most prominent approaches, and researchers propose analytic tools for helping disputants choose which model to use. Different authors organize their overview of mediation models differently, but three of the most prominent models that generally emerge as major players in the analyses are Interest-Based Mediation, Transformative Mediation, and Narrative Mediation. Each has its roots in a prominent philosophy or social theory that has been influential in North America over the past decades, and each has basic assumptions about conflict that give rise to distinctive styles and techniques of mediator intervention.

Interest-Based Mediation is perhaps the most widely used model. It is reflected in the works of authors like Roger Fisher, William Ury, and Christopher Moore, and it is used in business and in justice contexts where it is regarded as an efficient alternative to traditional legal procedures. The focus here is on settling disputes, reaching agreements, maximizing outcomes, and solving problems. It is rooted in a liberal philosophy associated with authors like John Rawls and Ronald Dworkin that focuses on individuals and their freely chosen interests. The goal of democratic society is maximizing freedom and equality for individuals. The mediator's goal is to help participants achieve a settlement that maximizes their interests, and the assumption is that collaborative interaction will yield better outcomes than competitive interactions. Mediator strategies aim at fostering collaboration, finding compromises, and engaging parties creatively in generating options that meet the needs of all. Mediations here are viewed as practical solutions to problems, and they aim at efficiency and effectiveness in problem solving.[48]

Transformative Mediation is quite different. Launched in 1994 by Robert Baruch Bush and Joseph Folger,[49] it reflects the communitarian social philosophy of authors like Robert Bellah, Michael Sandel, and Amitai Etzioni. Like their work, it is formulated as a critique of the individualism of liberal philosophy. The assumption of Transformative mediators is that people are not disconnected individuals with freely chosen interests. Rather, they are connected by cultures, traditions, religions, communities, and relationships. These connections are at the heart of what makes democracies healthy. Conflicts do not arise simply from the diversity of freely chosen interests; they arise because of deeper connections that need to be explored and lived out more responsibly.

In the Transformative model, conflict is principally about relationships. Mediators aim at building and restoring relationships because they believe that conflict creates discomfort and diverts parties from patterns of relating they would otherwise choose. Their assumption is that conflict forces parties into behaviours that alienate them from their own strengths and their connections with others. Conflict is viewed as an opportunity for moral growth and personal transformation. This means that focusing narrowly on problem solving and efficiency will not get to the heart of things.

With a mediator's help, parties can change the quality of conflict interaction by recapturing their sense of competence and connection with each other. This reverses the negative conflict cycle, and reestablishes a constructive interaction that enables them to move forward on a more positive footing. This is called conflict transformation, and the key words are 'empowerment' and 'recognition.' Transformative mediators are convinced that parties have both the desire and the capacity to make the necessary shifts to become more open to each other. They help parties do this by highlighting opportunities for shifts that surface from the parties' own stories. Empowerment and recognition cannot be forced, but neither can they be supplanted or ignored. Transformative mediators work by cultivating opportunities presented by the parties themselves.[50]

The third model, Narrative Mediation, was introduced in 2000 by John Winslade and Gerald Monk.[51] Like the other two models, it has its roots in a social philosophy: the social constructionist theory of authors like Kenneth Gergen and Vivien Burr. The assumption of Narrative Mediation is that conflicts arise, not simply because of problems, but because of the 'stories' that lie behind the parties' understanding of the problem and its social context. The mediator's goal is not to probe the facts of the dispute, but to help parties establish a relationship, deconstruct conflict-saturated stories, and produce an alternate story that incorporates elements of agreement and points of cooperation and mutual respect.

Narrative mediators assume that conflicts arise from participants' sense of themselves and others in relation to wider social processes. They are critical of problem-solving approaches that focus too narrowly on the 'facts' of the problem. Their assumption is that conflictual relations are a function of narratives that provide stories of past events, situate the present in relation to these stories, and project future possibilities in relation to them. Changing social relations requires changing the stories. But before new stories can be constructed, old conflict-laden stories must be deconstructed. Mediators use strategies that help parties raise questions about their stories and explore possibilities for new stories. Their assumption is that social relations are constructions of human meaning. Their effort, then, is to find new meaningful constructions that enable parties to get out of the limitations of conflict-laden pasts, and into the possibilities for new relationships embedded in new narratives.[52]

The diversity of mediation models presents an opportunity for people in conflict to choose mediators and mediation styles to suit their needs. Conflicts differ, as do their social contexts. The models provide a range of alternative intervention strategies as well as indicators for evaluating which approach and which mediator might prove helpful for dealing with a particular conflict. The conversations around mediation models, however, also present mediators and researchers with opportunities for asking deeper questions about their practices in relation to the dominant approaches. Do the models capture and reflect what I do? Are there things left unsaid by the models? What goes on when mediators help us work our way through conflicts? What is the role of learning in this process? What can we learn about learning that can help us to do this better?

Advancing Our Knowledge: Conflict, Learning, and Insight Theory

These questions bring us back to our line of inquiry on the role of learning in conflict and the Insight Theory of Lonergan. This overview of the study of conflict reveals a number of themes relevant to our inquiry. The first is that conflict can provide occasions for personal and social learning and growth. Learning the attitudes, tools, and skills for managing conflict cooperatively can help make it a productive part of life. The idea of learning here is central. What is interesting, however, is that the learning envisioned is not simply the learning of conflict management skills; it is also the personal learning and development of participants within conflict itself. We can learn in conflict and we can learn from conflict, and this learning can contribute to personal and organizational growth. Social and organizational life is not static; it is constantly changing. Dealing cooperatively with conflicts can provide occasions for development, and working through conflicts can provide the occasion for personal learning and growth in ideas, attitudes, and skills related to social life.

A second theme arises from Game Theory. Conflicts do not need to result in win-lose or violent outcomes; participants can learn cooperative approaches that can advance their own interests as well as the interests of others. In fact, it was this learning that arose in the iterations of Game Theory research that most attracted theorists. In a world where violence could spell the nuclear destruction of the planet, this was good news. Game theorists discovered that approaching conflict cooperatively need not be dismissed as dewy-eyed idealism. It could be supported by hard-nosed science, and it could be learned even by self-interested parties. Game Theory research brought to light the importance of this learning, and it established a climate of scientific research that embraced this sort of learning as a reasonable, practical objective.

Another theme arises from Interest Theory and Human Needs Theory. Conflict practitioners discovered that theory, textbooks, and computer models alone would not provide the tools required for this learning. The learning needs to be practice-based. Resolving conflicts requires distinguishing positions from interests and needs, and probing the deeper factors that underlie conflicts. This requires learning habits and skills, and un-learning dysfunctional habits, attitudes, ideologies, and assumptions. The learning needs to move from the realm of abstract principles to the world of concrete issues, personalities, strategies, social systems, and historical contexts.

Communication Theory reveals the complexity of this learning. Communication in conflicts is not simply the exchange of information, and conflicts are not simply the interaction of parties with defined interests or needs. The dynamics of conflict shape the parties and their sense of reality. The learning that breaks the grip of dysfunctional meanings in conflict must now submit to more complex analyses – analyses that capture both the personal and the social dynamics of the transformations that reshape conflicts.

With mediation arises another theme relevant to this inquiry. Conflict practitioners discovered that disputants need not face the challenges of conflicts on their own. Third-party mediators can provide assistance by guiding the process and facilitating communication when conflicts prove difficult. Mediators can develop and implement skills for helping disputants through the learning involved in conflicts. The implication here is that mediators can be involved in facilitating disputants' learning in conflicts. Can we think of mediators as learning facilitators? If so, then what does this involve? What can we learn about learning to help mediators do this work better?

The development of diverse mediation models provides the occasion for conversations about mediator goals, tasks, and strategies, and these conversations bring us to the role of Insight Theory in helping to understand the learning involved in conflicts. How can we better understand the learning observed by Game Theorists? What are the learning challenges confronted by conflict practitioners? Why is learning new skills and attitudes towards conflict so difficult? What kind of learning goes on when disputants shift from competitive to cooperative attitudes towards conflict? What really happens when the 'magic' in mediation occurs? These questions ask about the personal transformative moment in the learning process. How does this transformative learning happen? What does it involve, and how do mediators help make it happen? We believe that Insight Theory can help probe some of the fundamental questions arising in the history of conflict research.

Researchers and practitioners at Carleton University, Ottawa, have developed a practice-based research initiative that explores these questions. At the core of this project is a mediation model that has proven quite successful. Understanding this success, however, has brought conflict theorists and practitioners into dialogue with philosophers studying the work of Lonergan at Saint Paul University, Ottawa. The result is Insight Mediation, a learning-centred model that builds upon the twin pillars of practice and theory.[53] What we find is a wealth of ideas on the transformative moment in learning: how this learning requires a careful attention to the details of the conflict; how it carries the learner beyond the data to insights; how insight transforms feelings; how it alters perspectives and opens new possibilities for relationships; how it constructs narratives but also grounds them in a more realistic understanding of contexts and opportunities.[54] Insight Theory offers tools for understanding many aspects of conflict and conflict resolution.

Concluding Remarks

In the following chapters, we explore some of the results of these investigations. We believe the study of conflict has brought us to an important moment in history. Research and scholarship can, indeed, offer resources for helping deal more constructively with the conflicts that challenge our lives. We are interested in exploring the learning entailed in this work. This research, however, must move forward in close cooperation with the work of conflict practitioners. What practitioners recognize is that resolving conflicts is difficult, and it brings us face-to-face with difficult learning challenges that are intimately personal. We explore what some of this learning involves. Practitioner research can help resist the allure of elegant systems. It can also help support some important challenges to prevailing social theories that overemphasize the competitive character of society and the intractability of conflicts. Human societies involve cooperation, and cooperative approaches towards conflict can mark a shift in social attitudes. In the next chapter, we introduce Insight Theory, and in the chapters that follow, we explore how it can help answer some of these questions and develop some of these ideas.

3 Insight Theory: Transformation through Learning

Imagine a familiar scenario. You are in a conversation with a family member and, try as you might, you just cannot get her to understand. Something important is at stake, something that evokes strong feelings in you both and keeps you trying to explain yourselves. But you make little progress. The conversation turns into an argument, and soon enough things begin to degenerate into a pattern of conflict that is all too familiar. This time, however, something different happens. Something new occurs to you, and you stop talking. You begin wondering about something you had not thought of before. You look at her and ask: 'This is really important to you isn't it?' Then, to her surprise, you name what she cares about. Contrary to what she expects, there is no mockery or condescension in your voice, only respect and understanding. Most compelling, however, is that you got it right. She answers with appreciation. Something opens up in your feelings, and you begin talking differently. The familiar pattern of argument gives way to a real conversation.

This is a very ordinary experience, and events like it occur frequently in daily life. Like many experiences in life, its familiarity conceals considerable complexity. What is even more complex is the way our assumptions about the possibility of such outcomes shape the way we participate in conflicts generally. So often we despair of anything good coming from conflict, and this can be a self-fulfilling prophecy. This despair is linked to an implicit, but rarely acknowledged conviction that this is the way things should turn out, but alas, they seldom do. What is going on in this experience? What can be learned about this experience so that successful conflict resolution happens more often?

In this chapter, we introduce the Insight Theory of Lonergan by exploring some of the features of this experience and others like it. Before we begin, we would like to say a few words about this family conflict scenario and the way it is linked to the theme of the book. Our assumption is that this experience is genuine. Often enough, we experience unexpected shifts in conversations, only to discover later that the other person has been manipulating us. Our focus here is not on the manipulation experience, but on the genuine article. The reason is that we want to explore what happens in experiences like this that makes them significant for managing conflicts. Our belief is that assumptions about conflict shape the way we participate in personal and public life. Understanding what goes on in successful conflict resolution can clarify some of these assumptions and enhance our participation as family members and citizens.

We also begin with this scenario because it is familiar and provides a good starting point for exploring the links between Insight Theory and conflict resolution in the chapters that follow. The situation recounted above has a number of recognizable features. First, the conversation has become a conflict. And what is more familiar than a family conflict? Second, something happens to transform the conflict into a good conversation. It is this transformative moment that will be our point of focus in exploring insights. Third, the insight involves learning: discovering something new, or discovering the relevance of something forgotten. Our goal is to explore features of this learning. Fourth, experiences like this do not simply affect us as individuals, but they affect our relations with others. They shift the pattern of our relationships, and they have an effect that extends beyond the moment. Finally, because this experience transforms relationships, understanding more about it can enhance our understanding of conflict and the influence it has on democracy, justice, and interpersonal relations. Most issues arising in public life are far more complex than this family conflict portrays, and most extend beyond the intimate relations of family. Yet, in one way or another, social life is about conflicts and relationships. Understanding how insight can transform conflicts can play an important role in thinking through more complex problems. We begin with an explanation of Lonergan's method of self-understanding, a method that focuses on 'getting insight into insights.'

Lonergan's Method of Self-Understanding: Gaining Insight into Insights

Illustrations that evoke personal experiences are central to the method of self-understanding of Insight Theory.[1] A few words about this method are in order here. Lonergan's is not a typical philosophy. It is not a set of grand principles or axioms about the nature of things. Rather, it is a method of self-understanding. It involves a process of reflecting on ourselves as we go about our experiences of daily life. It is a type of 'reflective practice' in that it presupposes that we first learn how to do things in life and then only later do we get around to analysing what we are doing.[2] We learn to ride a bicycle before we learn the physics of bicycle riding. We learn to talk before studying grammar. We learn the practices of a profession before we develop the theories that explain them.

But Lonergan's method is different from standard examples of reflective practice in that its focus is particular. The focus of Insight Theory is our personal acts of understanding. Consider a simple example of a newspaper crossword puzzle. When we are puzzling through a particular word clue, our focus is on the clues, the word we are trying to discover, the number of letters, the location in the puzzle, and the links with the other words that intersect with it. Through all of this, we are performing a set of activities or operations: we are reading the newspaper, we are reading the clues, we are asking questions, we are trying on alternative answers, we arrive at insights, we test our insights to see whether they satisfy all the conditions of the puzzle, we verify our answers, we decide to write them in, and we go on to other words. All of these are operations, and together they make up the process of understanding, in this case, the understanding required to solve the puzzle.

Normally, we do not focus on these operations; we simply perform them. Our focus is on the problem the puzzle poses. Yet we do 'experience' our operations of understanding as we perform them. Our awareness is not simply an awareness of the puzzle, it also includes an awareness of ourselves doing the puzzle. This self-awareness does not mean we understand ourselves fully, but it does mean that our activity of ourselves doing the puzzle falls within our field of experience. We can pay attention to this experience, wonder about it, ask questions about it, and get insights into what we are doing. As with other instances of reflective practice, it is possible to develop an ability to do crossword puzzles with a double focus of attention: the first on solving the puzzle, the second on the operations we are performing in solving the puzzle. This double focus of attention is at the core of the method of Insight Theory. When we cultivate the skills involved in this self-attention, we become capable of understanding the operations we use in working through the puzzle. The result is an ability to discern and distinguish the various operations that transform us in the learning process. Most important is the ability to catch ourselves in the act of insight.

At the centre of Lonergan's philosophy is the act of insight. We can all recall personal instances of 'aha' experiences, and dramatic stories of insight are the stuff of legends. Archimedes is famous for his insight experience in the bath, and stories are told of how Isaac Newton's insight was prompted by an apple falling on his head. Yet, as notable as insights are, they stubbornly resist being examined and understood. This is because they are often emotionally charged. They draw our attention towards the things we are trying to understand and away from ourselves in the act of understanding. The struggle towards insight requires considerable concentration, and when insights occur, the new meanings they reveal grab our attention. It is difficult to engage the double focus of attention of reflective practice when we are being buffeted about by the emotional dynamics of insight. Still, it is not impossible, and it can be developed with practice. We experience ourselves as actors in the insight process, and this self-experience can be cultivated into a focused self-attention. When we do this, we become capable of observing features of insight that otherwise go unnoticed. We begin observing insights, how they work, and how they transform conversations. We begin noticing how they can shape the course of conflicts towards resolution, and how they can be facilitated by mediators. Attention to insights can become part of the training of conflict practitioners.

There is another reason why insights frequently go unanalysed. This is because they involve a shift in us from one inner state of meaning to another, a shift that is often so complete it is difficult to pay attention to the transformation process itself. Before the insight, we cannot imagine what it is like to understand, and after the insight, we find it difficult to remember what it was like not to understand. To observe the transformation process requires that we carefully record experiential data on both the 'before' and 'after' states. It requires that we evoke the experience often so as to cultivate a habit of observing the shift from 'before' to 'after.' Insight Theory requires developing the ability to get past this blockage, to pay careful attention to the transformation process, so we can observe and understand the insight itself.

Another problem is the influence of standard images. Typically, when asked to describe insights, we turn to images like assembling parts into wholes, turning on light bulbs, or constructing narratives.

Careful examination of real insights, however, reveals that these images can be quite misleading. Before an insight, we do not have parts. We do not know what counts as a part because we do not know how the data are going to relate. We do not know which data are relevant, and in many cases we do not even know what counts as data. All we 'have' before the insight is a confused mass of 'stuff.' The idea of parts only emerges after we get the whole. So too with the image of the lightbulb. The image suggests that, in some way, the order of the room is 'there' before the lightbulb is turned on and the light simply allows us to 'see.' The fact is that, before an insight, there is no order, there is only confusion, and the only things we 'have' are questions and possible hunches as to where order might be discovered. Similarly with the image of constructing a narrative – we do not construct insights. In some curious way, they happen to us, we receive them, they arrive unexpectedly. To be sure, we can push the analogy so that writing stories comes to appear similar to gaining insights. It is the word 'construct' that is misleading. Insights involve a curious combination of active pursuit and passive reception. An accurate understanding of insight requires careful attention to real insights, and this means having a method for self-understanding.

Conflict makes it doubly difficult to focus attention on our own operations of insight. Heightened emotions have the effect of concentrating our concern outward towards the issues and people that challenge us. The insights that occur in conflict arise quickly, and they draw us into them, carrying us forward within their drama, shaping and reshaping our sense of ourselves and others. Here is where third parties can be helpful. When mediators have learned the skills of understanding their own operations of questioning and insight, they can identify more accurately these operations in others. They can help parties gain self-understanding, and can help them become curious about the cares and concerns of others.

Something else is difficult about the method of self-understanding. Struggling towards insights can draw us into battles with self-esteem. Frequently insight activities evoke feelings of fear that we will fail, that we will never 'get it,' that we will be found to be 'stupid,' that we will be made an object of ridicule. These feelings often arise quite dramatically when insight exercises are done in a group context or a classroom setting. 'Who will be the first to get it?' 'Who will be last?' 'What if I never get it?' It is as if being asked to get insights takes us back to elementary school, to our most traumatic memories of public humiliation.

Even when we are quick, our preoccupation with being quick can divert our attention away from self-understanding. These problems of self-esteem are not reserved for group learning contexts; they also badger us in our solitude and in conflicts with others. What if I am wrong? What if I cannot defend myself? What if I give in like I always do? It can be extremely difficult to move our attention away from feelings of anxiety and expected humiliation that accompany self-insight to focus on observing and understanding the operations themselves. Learning theorists have devoted considerable attention to the self-esteem barriers encountered in the learning process.[3]

Still and all, the obstacles to the method of self-understanding are not insurmountable. It is possible to develop an ability to pay attention to our operations of understanding, to observe their features, to discover how they work, and to verify our discoveries through publicly sharing and critically evaluating results with others. In the following pages, we focus on introducing key ideas that come out of this method, and exploring how they can be helpful in understanding and resolving conflict. As we go along, we provide examples to illustrate the method in action. We begin by exploring some features of Lonergan's Insight Theory.[4]

Insight Theory: The Curious Nature of Insight

Many of the features of Insight Theory are curious, and one of the most curious involves the relationship between pursuing insights and gaining them.[5] There is something active and something passive about insights. Insights are answers to questions, and normally they do not occur unless we pursue them actively in a process of questioning, studying the data, and looking for clues. But achieving insights is never fully under our control. Often they elude us. We must wait for them, positioning ourselves in readiness. We stumble upon them. They happen to us, and we receive them when they arrive. Sometimes they arrive like a bolt out of the blue sky.

We can cultivate the skills of questioning and working through problems in selected activities and fields. We can increase the likelihood of insights so that, for example, with specific types of puzzles, insights eventually come as a matter of course. But at other times, they are not so easily controlled. Sometimes we must wait quite a long time: days, months, even years. Sometimes they occur in our sleep, or in the morning, or in the shower, or driving to work, or while doing routine activities. Sometimes insights come when we least expect them, after we have put the problem aside and shifted our attention elsewhere. Sometimes they do not come at all. To be sure, we can practise in specific areas and improve our skill. But even then, there are times when we are stumped. And when that happens, we must wait for the insights to arrive in their own good time. Insights involve both active pursuit and passive reception. This is why the image of 'constructing' knowledge can be misleading.

Linked to this is the element of surprise. Insights often catch us unawares, and they leave us feeling a little amazed. To be sure, we become used to the small insights that occur all the time. We usually develop something of an immunity to this feeling of surprise. Yet, the bigger insights never cease to break through and catch us off guard. If we pay close attention, we can even retrieve something of this element of surprise in the smaller insights. Insights surprise us partly because they arrive unexpectedly. But they also surprise us because of what they do to us. Insights transform us from confusion to comprehension. Before the insight, we are confused; after, we understand. It is as simple as that. This transformation in our state of understanding is always something of a 'jump-shift.' It can involve a gradual transition, but it is never the sort of transition where we 'see clearly' where we are headed. Even when insights sneak up on us over time, the final transition usually leaves us with a feeling of having been transported or relocated. We can reconstruct the journey afterwards, but in the confusion prior to insight, the path is never clear.[6]

This shift from confusion to comprehension is the heart of learning. Yet, it is the part of learning least understood. We believe we should be able to chart the course of learning. We speak of setting learning goals, laying out strategies, and taking control of the learning process. Yet there is something about insight that defies our good intentions and thwarts our efforts to plan the route from not-knowing to knowing. Getting insights requires that we pursue them. But it also requires that we let ourselves be caught unawares by them. It requires being open to surprise, the surprise of being transported into something that, before it happens, we cannot imagine. It requires setting the map aside and giving ourselves over to the state of un-knowing.

It is this element of surprise and unpredictability that helps explain the stress experienced by professionals who must get insights in situations involving danger. Physicians, aircraft mechanics, and conflict mediators often find themselves dealing with situations where the consequences of failure can be serious: patients can die; people can be injured or killed in accidents; family relationships can be destroyed and children harmed; nations can go to war. The professionals have been charged with the task of discerning problems and facilitating solutions. Yet, discernment requires insight, and insight can never be brought totally under our control. We cannot predict fully whether or when we will gain insights. When professionals like mediators have the responsibility of facilitating insights in others, the challenges become doubly complicated. What makes matters worse is that, before the insights, we have no clear idea where they will lie. We have the lessons learned from prior cases. We have theories and strategies for trying things out and verifying possible options. Yet we do not know which lessons, which theories, which strategies, or which cases will prove helpful in this instance. The only way to find out is to plunge into the unknown. This can be quite stressful.

Still, the stress of the unknown is also the excitement of the unknown. And no unknown is more exciting than ... well ... the things we do not know. This excitement is part of the allure of good art and literature. We come to know many of the important things of our lives through books, theatre, films, art, music, and dance. When these involve real understanding, rather than simply remembering words and replaying images, they involve insights. These may not be the problem-solving insights typically associated with intellectual puzzles,[7] but they are insights nonetheless. We celebrate the authors and artists that help us achieve a more profound understanding of ourselves. Good artists steer readers, viewers, and listeners along new paths, they open up new experiential vistas, and they recreate the drama of these experiences. They set up alternative clues and anticipations, and usher in new ways of imagining. When they do their work well, they set the conditions for insight, and readers, viewers, and listeners come away feeling the gifts brought by these insights.

One of the distinctive features of Insight Theory is that it explains the learning process as involving a series of different types of operations, each with its own characteristics. Lonergan identifies four groups of operations: *experience, understanding, verification,* and *decision*.[8] In order to gain insights, we need to have *experiences*. We need to hear, taste, smell, feel, and see. Sometimes this requires learning to pay attention in new ways. We need to immerse ourselves in experiential contexts and cultivate ever new forms of awareness.

But experiencing something is not the same as *understanding* it. We can see an object and not know what it is. We can hear another's words and fail to understand their meaning. Understanding requires getting insights that apprehend an intelligibility or a meaning in experience that is not discernible prior to insight. To achieve insight requires questions. Insights do not float in mid-air; they are answers to questions. Different lines of questioning set the inquiry process moving in different directions, some more fruitful than others. The insights that yield the meanings that answer questions are called direct insights. These are the 'aha!' experiences that transform us from confusion to understanding. To achieve direct insights, however, often requires moving back and forth among different lines of questioning. Sometimes we discover that if we want to understand a person's meaning, we need to shift our line of questioning. Our questions can be on the wrong track, and we can discover that this is so. These discoveries are called inverse insights. On their own, they do not answer our questions, but they do put us on a new road towards understanding another's meaning. They do their work by detaching us from dead-end lines of inquiry. Once on the new path, we can gain direct insights that answer our questions.

But the learning process does not end here because our insights can be mistaken. To move forward in the process requires *verification*. Here we reflect back upon our direct insights to determine whether they make sense of our experiences and satisfy all the conditions set by our questions. Learning is not a linear process, it involves looping back again and again, returning to our experiences, questions, and insights with questions for verification, asking whether all the conditions are met for pronouncing them reliable.

Finally, for the learning process to culminate in action, we need to make *decisions*. Here our questioning asks us to take a stand, to become involved personally in new ways, to carry our reflection forward into action. Once again, the process is not linear, it involves looping back to experience, understanding, and verification, now with questions about values. In the pages that follow, we explore some of the features of each of these groups of operations, particularly as they arise in conflict.

The Role of Experiences and Questions in the Learning Process

Sometimes we see or hear things and immediately understand them. At other times, we do not. Learning requires more than seeing and hearing; it requires insight, and Insight Theory makes a distinction between sensory experience and getting the insights that yield understanding. Even when we understand things quickly, there are two things going on in the same moment: sensory experience and insight. Insight Theory invites us to distinguish between them. When experiences are not followed immediately by understanding, we ask questions, and learning requires following the questions that lead us to the direct insights that answer our questions.

What is interesting is that insights, once achieved, reshape the way we experience the sensory data the next time around. Once we understand the first time, we usually do not need to go through the same laborious process again. All we need is to encounter the experience and voilà! we get it immediately. This is why learning a new language, as difficult as it is in the initial stages, becomes easier as we go along. Insights, once achieved, leave their imprint on subsequent experiences. This means that today's experiences are laden with meanings that are the result of the direct insights from the past. The result is that there is a two-fold relationship between experience and insight. Experiences precede insights and provide the grounds for them. But our experiences are also transformed by our insights, and so they flow out of insights and are shaped by them.

The key to understanding the relationship between insight and experience lies in the questions asked. Insights are more than simply imaginative constructions; they are answers to questions. Questions arise from experience, and they ask about patterns or relations in our experience. Before we gain answers, the materials we work with in the inquiry process are our experiences. Once insights occur, they enter into our habitual pattern of experience to supply the materials for the next round of questions. Experience, as it is understood in Insight Theory, is experience-with-respect-to-questions. It is experience as illuminated by the light of questioning. It sets the stage for our questioning, it provides the data for our probing, hunching, and imagining, and it supplies the materials that are integrated and related in our insights.

Preparing ourselves for insight can be an elaborate affair. Learning about other cultures can require immersing ourselves in the experiences, routines, neighbourhoods, families, and prayer life of that culture. Without these experiences, we would not get the insights. We would not even know what questions to ask. This can involve living among them for extended periods of time. The professional training of airline pilots, counsellors, and social workers also involves long periods of immersion in new experiences under the guidance of mentors. Learning in the natural sciences requires significant inculturation into the experiential routines, habits, attitudes, and methods of data gathering and empirical verification of the field. Insights are not arbitrary constructions of the mind. They arise from experiences, and they only answer the questions of a given field when the learner is immersed in the experiences appropriate to that field.

Learning also requires curiosity. Getting insights requires questions, and at times, it requires that we shift from one line of questioning to another. Questions direct the inquiry process, and they do so by being both open-ended and also quite focused. Questions ask about specific things, they point in specific directions, they aim somewhere, and they provide indicators of what can count as answers, but on their own, they do not specify their goals. Rather, they head us towards the open vistas that remain unknown. We ask questions precisely because we do not know the answers, and the questions we ask aim at these unknowns. Our curiosity sends the inquiry process heading down particular roads, in search of particular sets of experiences. Still, on their own, our questions do not know their goals. They must await insights. Questions presuppose contexts, frames of reference, or horizons that are defined by sets of prior insights, yet on their own, they only aim towards their objects with the hope that the direction they provide eventually leads to insights. Curiosity and questioning play a significant role in resolving conflicts, and in the next chapter, we explore how Insight mediators develop strategies for helping parties shift lines of questioning when they become stuck in conflict. One of the most important resources of mediators is curiosity, and they are most helpful when they help parties develop their own curiosity about the cares and concerns of others.

What questions do provide are the criteria that insights must meet if they are to qualify as answers.[9] This is how we learn that insights are, indeed, answers to our questions. It is also how we search for answers. Questions direct our attention in light of these criteria, and they tell us when we have found answers that meet them. So, for example, the rules and clues of a crossword puzzle provide direction in the search for answers. They tell us how many letters the word must have, some features of its meaning, and how its letters must be shared by other words in the puzzle. Similarly, in conversations, understanding another person often involves questions for clarification. These questions indicate the words that give rise to confusion or the gestures that seem to contradict how we have understood their words. They locate the source of the confusion and provide us with indicators of how it might be clarified. The questions provide direction in our efforts to understand them. Questions about personal feelings guide the conversation away from abstract ideas towards things that matter to them and events that have affected them. Gaining insights in conflicts requires asking questions about feelings and directing inquiry in search of the cares and concerns that lie behind the feelings. Curiosity and questioning have this odd combination of being both open-ended and focused. They provide criteria that direct us in search of insights while remaining open to new discoveries.

Being curious often involves shifting back and forth among various lines of questioning in order to get an accurate perspective. This is particularly so when our learning involves understanding other people. We need to understand the frames of reference that shape their perspective. This requires discovering the experiences that are important for them and the frameworks for interpreting these experiences. Sometimes, the real challenge of understanding others is making sense of these perspectives or reference frames. This is what we look for when we ask: 'Where are you coming from?' 'Where is all this anger coming from?' or 'What makes you think that about me?' These questions ask about reference frames. The questions work by aiming at unknowns, but they direct this aim and focus attention on interpretive frameworks. Understanding others means getting the line of questioning that helps us understand the frameworks that make sense of their words and gestures.

The complex relations among experiences, questions, and insights makes learning a very rich affair indeed. Today's insights answer today's questions, but they also enter into our habitual way of experiencing the world tomorrow. More than this, they become part of the experiential basis for tomorrow's efforts to answer new questions. In this way, insights build upon prior insights, and our experiences become a compound product of sensory perceptions and prior insights. But the compound character of experience also complicates things. To answer a question correctly often requires scrutinizing our experience and sorting out whether the images that have been evoked are relevant. Did I hear music or did I hear a child crying? Is he being serious or is he mocking me? Our experiences include the auditory or visual perceptions, but they also evoke images and memories of prior meanings that were the product of prior understandings. Sorting through these layers often becomes difficult, for example, when events in our adult lives trigger strong feelings from childhood experiences. We do not always know if these prior meanings and feelings are reliable data for today's questioning, and sifting through these layers of experience can play an important role in the learning involved in conflicts.

Fortunately, the compound, multilayered character of experience also means we can check things out. We can move ourselves closer to the source of the sound. We can watch people's faces more carefully for signs of mockery. We can dig deeper through the layers of experience to access further data in search of correlations and confirmations. We do not always do this. And getting beyond preconceived notions is often a difficult affair. Still, it is not impossible. We can check things out, and we can know we have been mistaken. Sometimes we can even correct our mistakes. Because of the compound character of experience, we have access to multiple layers of data. Listening, watching, noticing, attending carefully, and exploring new lines of questioning can lead us to layers of data that reveal flaws in our more casual observations. In this way, we can move beyond more hastily formulated impressions towards deeper learning about ourselves and others.

One final note. Insight requires genuine curiosity and genuine questioning. It requires admitting that we do not already know the answers, and sometimes this can require considerable discipline and humility. We cannot give ourselves over to the process of inquiry fully and freely if we are convinced we already know. It requires trust in the inquiry process. Many of us who have been called 'stupid' too often by parents, teachers, and peers do not sit comfortably with the state of not-knowing. Our culture has made ignorance a shameful thing and this is a terrible tragedy. The road to insight can only begin with the willing acceptance of not-knowing. The principle engine of learning is the curiosity that draws us forward in questioning towards insight. Without the calm acceptance of the state prior to knowing, this curiosity has difficulty taking hold.

The Direct Insight: The 'Aha' Moment of the Learning Process

Two types of insight occur in the learning process: direct and inverse. The direct insight is the most familiar, and it is the most important operation in the process. Inverse insights are less well-known, and they involve a rather strange type of understanding that has attracted less attention, even among Lonergan scholars. Lonergan's analyses of direct and inverse insight are among his most powerful and innovative contributions to philosophy. We argue that both types of insight are of central importance to the field of conflict and conflict resolution. In the next chapter, we explore two strategies of Insight Mediation associated with direct and inverse insights: linking and de-linking.

We begin with the direct insight.[10] This is the 'aha' event that answers our questions, transforms us from confusion to understanding, and gives rise to the meanings that enrich our experiences. One of the reasons why direct insights are so misunderstood has to do with the curious relation between the 'inner' experience of insights and our sense of the 'outer' world that is shaped and transformed by them. We often use the word 'see' to describe insights. But there is an important sense in which this word is quite misleading. Seeing with our eyes does not involve getting insights because insights require more than simply taking a look. Direct insights are inner experiences of meaning that require questioning, pursuing clues, examining data, probing feelings, and hitting on answers. They involve an experience of transformation in our world of meaning that is deeply personal, deeply inward, and deeply felt. Yet, in spite of this, it is also true that direct insights transform our sense of the outer world. They shape and reshape the way we see, hear, and feel the world. There is something profoundly extroverted about them that restructures our sense of the world around us. Insights are profoundly inner, and they constitute our sense of the outer world.

This curious relation between the inner and outer dimensions of direct insight is one of the reasons why teaching is so difficult and learning is so often misunderstood. When we have insights, we assume they are 'visible' in the data of experience, and so we think they are equally accessible to others. We find it hard to understand why others do not 'see' as we do. Consequently, our standard teaching strategies often involve assembling materials and directing attention to the elements we consider important. We honestly believe that if the materials are properly displayed, others will understand them as we do. The fact is, however, nothing could be further from the truth. Understanding is not 'seeing.' Others will not understand as we do if they have not travelled the personal road from questions, through data, clues, and hunches, to insights. Teaching requires helping others along this personal road of discovery and learning.

There is another layer of complexity to this relation between the inner and outer dimensions of direct insight. Once we gain insights, they settle into our habitual landscape of experience and become 'invisible' as acts of insight. They only appear 'visible' as objects of experience. When we look at an electric lamp, for instance, we think we are 'seeing' the lamp. The fact is, however, we have forgotten that to know the lamp as a lamp, we had to learn a great deal: we had to understand something about electricity, light bulbs, the challenges of stumbling around in the dark, and the intricacies of fashion. All of these required insights at some point in our lives. Trying to explain the lamp to a citizen of a culture that has not had these insights would be a mighty difficult affair. The same is true when we read printed words on a page. When we know the language, we think we are 'seeing' the meaning. However, all we need do is try the same with a text in another language and we are forced to admit that to read requires insight. The problem is that insights settle into our habitual landscape of experience and become 'invisible' as operations of understanding. We think of them only as part of the 'outer' world of experience. Understanding the transformative learning of Insight Theory requires dismantling these habitual notions and replacing them with more complex understandings gained from careful attention to insight.

Mediators who follow Insight Theory can develop habits and skills for attending to parties' operations of experience and direct insight in conflicts. They cultivate an appreciation for the way a party's experience is often laden with prior insights that have become 'invisible.' With their own curiosity and non-judgmental questioning, mediators can probe parties' statements and reactions and help them gain insight into the meanings and interpretations that have become embedded in their habitual ways of experiencing others. When parties overcome obstacles created by hidden meanings, they often become curious and take control of the learning that leads them successfully through the resolution process.

The Inverse Insight: Changing Directions When We Can't Get There from Here

There is another type of operation involved in the understanding process that involves an odd, inverse type of activity.[11] Here we do not get answers to questions; rather, we discover that we are asking the wrong questions. Inverse insights mark the transition to entirely new ways of inquiring. They call for new ways of asking questions. They involve the discovery that 'you can't get there from here!'

One of the often celebrated features of the history of science is what Thomas Kuhn has called 'paradigm shifts.'[12] These are the dramatic shifts in scientific theories that usher in radical changes in the way science is done. Among the most remarkable of these was the revolution in physics introduced by Galileo and Newton. What is curious about their discoveries is that they not only introduced new ways of answering questions in physics, they also introduced new ways of asking questions. They discovered that the old ways of asking questions needed to be abandoned if physical phenomena were to be explained properly. Their major discoveries involved inverse insights. And these inverse insights marked a shift to a new way of questioning and learning that led to a host of new insights in the physical sciences.

Prior to Galileo and Newton, physics was dominated by questions that had seemed to make sense at the time and that can still seem to make sense today.[13] For example, when we throw a ball into the air, we watch it leave our hand, rise in the air, eventually slow down, and fall to the earth. The explanation that had prevailed since Aristotle was that this motion was to be explained in terms of the transfer and dissipation of impetus. The ball begins at rest, our hand imparts an impetus, this impetus is used up or dissipated through the motion of the ball, and it falls to earth when the impetus is finally spent. Given these common-sense notions, the logical line of questioning was to ask about this impetus: how is it transferred? how is it used up? how is it measured? These are the sorts of questions that had marked the history of physics to this point.

What Galileo and Newton discovered was that this line of questioning about impetus was all wrong. They had been experimenting in an effort to measure impetus, but none of the calculations added up. Something was wrong, not simply with the answers, but with the questions. There was something about the motion of the ball as it slowed down and returned to earth that could not be explained adequately in terms of the impetus theory. Instead of asking about the dissipation of impetus, they proposed that we begin asking about the intervention of other forces. Instead of thinking of the ball's natural state as the state of rest, they proposed asking whether its natural state might better be understood as a state of continued motion. The question for physics, then, would be why the ball does not simply keep going – forever!

Their inverse insight led to the discovery of inertial motion. Their discovery was that the natural state of objects is not rest but inertial motion, and inertial motion does not need to be explained in terms of the continued presence of forces. The question that physics needed to answer was why objects change motion: why they slow down, speed up, or change direction. Questions about the origin and dissipation of impetus do not help explain physical motion; they are a dead-end street. Their discovery was that earlier physical scientists were barking up the wrong tree. What followed was a series of new direct insights and a new path of learning in physics built upon Newton's explanatory theory of motions. What marked the shift was the inverse insight that pronounced the earlier line of questioning to be faulty.

Another example of inverse insight is provided by Lavoisier's discovery of oxidation.[14] Scientists in the late seventeenth and early eighteenth centuries were convinced that the burning of wood and candles was to be explained in terms of a substance called phlogiston. The common-sense supposition of the time was that materials that burned were composed of phlogiston, and burning was the release of the phlogiston that was trapped inside. Scientific experiments sought to capture the products of burning with the assumption that if all the gases derived from the burning and all the ash left behind could be weighed, they would equal the original mass of the unburnt materials. The gases would represent the phlogiston released, and the ash would represent the materials combined with phlogiston in the wood or candle wax. Since candles burned with no ash, the supposition was they were pure phlogiston.

Lavoisier's experiments produced astonishing results that led him to reject the entire line of questioning of phlogiston theory. What he found was that, in some experiments, when all the gases and ash were weighed after burning, the total mass was greater than the original unburnt materials. How could this be? His response was to suggest that the line of questioning was all wrong. Instead of asking what is released in burning, he proposed that we ask what is added. His discovery was an inverse insight. We had been asking the wrong questions. He proposed that burning is a process that combines solid materials with a special type of air. He went on to perform experiments with various kinds of airs, and eventually the name, oxygen, was given to that particular air or gas that combined with materials in burning. His new line of questioning led to the differentiation of diverse types of elements and compounds and the explanation of diverse phenomena in terms of chemical reactions. At the centre of his discovery, however, was the inverse insight that marked the shift to a new way of asking questions in chemistry.

These are spectacular examples of inverse insights. But many inverse insights are quite ordinary. How often do we come upon adverse situations looking for someone to blame, only to discover that the situation is not about blame? As parents, we run into this sort of thing all the time. Our expectation is that the situation involves someone at fault, usually one of the children, and so our questioning launches us in search of the culprit. What we discover is that our questioning is on the wrong track; the situation has been caused by something else entirely. We do not yet know the cause, but we find evidence that we have been barking up the wrong tree. So we begin a new path of learning based upon new kinds of questions. On its own, the inverse insight does not supply the cause; what it does is redirect the questioning to a search for a different type of cause.

Other examples arise when we try fixing machines. How often have we searched for the cause of a problem, only to discover that its origin might be sought in a completely different part of the machine? The car does not start and so we check out the battery and the starting system. We spend hours diagnosing, testing, maybe even replacing parts, but nothing adds up. All of a sudden we get an inverse insight. We need to begin looking elsewhere. We begin thinking 'outside the box.' Isn't the fuel system also involved in starting the car? What about those computers that always cost so much? And don't some of these cars have those devices that won't let your car start if some lever or switch is out of position? On its own, the inverse insight does not discover the cause. What it does is shift our line of questioning and open up new paths of learning.

Conversations are often the occasion for inverse insights. How often do we enter mid-way into conversations and jump to conclusions about another's comments, only to discover that the conversation is not about us? Our first expectations lead us to question the other person, to challenge them, to defend ourselves. But we get an inverse insight. The discussion is about something else entirely. Our feelings of indignation give way to curiosity, and we begin looking for clues and information that can help us learn what the conversation is about.

All of these involve inverse insights. On their own, they do not answer our questions. They do not tell us what caused the adverse situation, what caused the failure of the machine, or what the conversation was about. What they do tell us is that our prior lines of questioning were mistaken. You can't get there from here. Once released from mistaken lines of inquiry, we shift to other questions that eventually can lead to answers. This shift in our line of questioning is what is achieved by inverse insights.

What inverse insights do is de-link us from an attachment to questions and expectations that capture and focus our attention. It is not unusual to be preoccupied in specific ways, and normally this preoccupation highlights certain experiences and screens out others. This happens often in conflicts. When things matter to us, our attention is focused in ways that have been defined by prior insights and experiences, and this directs our questions, our expectations, and our interpretations of others. Negative experiences from the past often provide the framework for interpreting others. Continued questioning only exacerbates the conflict. Try as we might, we get nowhere. When we do break out, it is often because an inverse insight has intervened to de-link us from prior preoccupations. Once freed, we can become curious about other aspects of the problem that previously we had ignored or screened out. Our new-found questions and expectations can lead to new insights into the cares and concerns of others. The key to shifting gears is the inverse insight.

Verifying Insights: Asking the 'Is it So?' Question

Sometimes an insight provides the key that unlocks the door to understanding. At other times, however, it does not. Insights can be wrong. Insights mark an important moment in the learning process, but by themselves they are incomplete. To complete the process, they must be verified, and verification marks the next operation along the way.[15] Here we want to verify our answers; we want to know whether our direct insights are correct. Acts of verification share many of the features of direct insights: they arrive in their own good time, and they often take us by surprise. But they also have their own character and structure. Because so many conflicts involve misunderstandings, verification plays an important role in mediation and conflict resolution.

Acts of verification do not provide new insights; rather, they involve a different posture, a different attitude towards insights – an attitude of evaluation and judgment that asks, 'Is it so?' They involve a distinctive line of questioning that scrutinizes existing insights in search of evidence, and they play an important role of their own in the overall process of understanding.

Let us examine a simple illustration. Is it raining outside? This is a question that presupposes a prior question ('What's the weather?') and a direct insight that proposes an answer ('It is raining'). It asks for evidence either for or against the proposed candidate. It invites a different line of inquiry than, say, a question about the nature of rain. It supposes that we have some common-sense definition of rain as something like 'wet-from-the-sky,' and asks whether evidence can be found for rain here and now. The question can be answered in a number of ways: we can go outside to determine whether we can feel wet-from-the-sky; we can look out the window for visible signs of rain; or we can turn on the radio to check out the weather report. In each case, verification grasps the links between the question, the proposed answer, and the experiential evidence. Yes, we did indeed go outside and felt wet-from-the-sky; yes, we did look out the window and saw evidence of rain; yes, we turned on the radio and heard the report that confirmed rain all day today. Our judgment was that the evidence gained from feeling, seeing, or hearing verified the proposed answer.

Since the dawn of the scientific revolution, verification has caused endless problems. Early scientists had trouble with church officials for verifying that the motion of the earth with respect to the sun and planets was different from what had been commonly thought. A massive philosophical debate ensued about whether or how the sciences know 'reality.' In our age, we have come full circle. Now the claims of science are under critical scrutiny again, and this time the guardians of doctrine are philosophers and social scientists. Their concerns are with power and domination. They urge us to be suspicious about people who claim to know 'the truth' about 'the real world.'

The fact is, however, we verify our insights and make reliable judgments about 'the real' all the time. When we learn we have been wrong, we do so on the basis of other acts of verification that we presume correct. Even when we begin questioning all of our acts of verification, our suspicion is prompted by some discovery or theory we have judged to be reliable. Working through the nest of issues related to these debates is an arduous affair. There is a good deal of literature written on Insight Theory that engages these discussions, and it would be impossible to present it all here.[16] Our goal is different. We believe Insight Theory has much to offer the study of conflict, and we stand to gain from a relatively simple presentation of its basic ideas. Our goal in these chapters is to stick with the method of offering verifiable observations from ordinary experience, and to leave the more complex philosophical debates for another time and place.

Like direct and inverse insights, verification often goes unnoticed. When driving a car we double-check our mirror to determine whether the coast is clear to pass. We check our bank statements to verify whether our account balances are correct. We look both ways before crossing the street. We consult multiple sources of information to verify whether we have received good advice from professionals or salespersons. In conflicts, we ask questions to clear up misunderstandings. In each case, our search is not for new insights; it is the reflective search for evidence to affirm or overturn proposed answers to questions. This is an ordinary part of the learning process.

The key to verification is understanding how questions and insights establish the criteria or conditions that have to be met if the insights are to be pronounced true or false. Common-sense questions about rain are not very demanding. They simply require experiential evidence of 'wet-from-the-sky.' The same holds true for the judgments we make driving a car, checking our bank balance, crossing the street, verifying advice, and working through conflicts. Sciences like meteorology or medicine are another matter. What makes these sciences different is the precision of their questions, the demands established for gathering data, the technical horizons that specify the precise meanings of terms, and the requirement that data be correlated with other data and theory in service of broader, more comprehensive explanations. Ordinary life verification does not demand these same standards, although, at times, they do make an appeal to more technical judgments. This is when things can get complicated. Distinguishing between the common-sense and the technical components of verification can help in clearing up confusion when such complications arise.

Common-sense verification in our day-to-day relations with others is quite ordinary. It involves formulating our insights and the questions they are meant to answer; clarifying the criteria or conditions implied in our insights and questions to determine what data would need to be observed in order to pronounce them correct; checking out the data to determine whether the criteria or conditions are indeed fulfilled; and pronouncing accordingly on the insights. We perform these learning operations all the time. Verification can involve a resort to power and authority, but usually this is neither necessary nor helpful. The operations of verifying insights are open to the involvement of everyone, and parties in conflict can check for themselves the steps that others followed in verification. Like direct and inverse insights, acts of verification implicate our self-esteem, and this always adds a layer of complexity. Yet, the challenges of assuring the transparency and accessibility of verification in ordinary life are not insurmountable. We suggest that understanding the operations involved in verification can prove helpful in meeting some of these challenges, particularly when trying to resolve conflicts.

The Role of Feelings and Values in Insight Theory

There is a very interesting aspect of Insight Theory that concerns feelings and values.[17] Values are what matter to us, what we care about; they are what animate our lives, what define the way we are interested in the world. They may be deeply personal, but they are seldom merely personal. They speak about the world and our relations with others. They embrace commonly held ideas about the world, how it ought to be, and how we ought to live with others. They may express straightforward, pragmatic goals, or they may involve longer-term visions of society, history, or humanity. Values say something about where things are going and where we believe they ought to go. They define a direction, a trajectory, a path that present and future events ought to take. They call us to action, and they inform our deliberations in the direction of this trajectory. They frequently make appeals to past events, and they express themselves in relation to this past. Something important happened in the past to bring about the present. Values recall this past, and call us to move towards the future in a direction defined by this past.

Insight Theory invites us to observe four different ways of relating to values. These four ways are rooted in the different groups of operations of the learning process discussed earlier in this chapter. You will recall these are experiencing, understanding, verification, and decision. Insight Theory speaks of these groups of operations as levels, because they tend to operate cumulatively, each building upon the previous operations within a circular process in which verification and decision lead to new experiencing and new understanding. Although they operate cumulatively, they do not function in a linear or a temporally defined sequence. We frequently circle back and forth through the groups of operations, later operations reshaping our engagement in earlier ones, and earlier ones providing resources that are carried forward and developed in later operations in the learning process.

At a first level, we experience values. We notice them operating within our own lives and the lives of others. We may not give them much thought, nor do we always know what they are about, or where they come from. Still, we do encounter values, and the principal feature of this encounter is the experience of desire, aversion, attraction, or repulsion. We experience values as feelings. This may be a straightforward matter of desiring to drive to work instead of walking. Or it may involve more complex feelings of being drawn towards a life career or away from people we feel cannot be trusted. Experiencing values is not restricted to our own desires and feelings; it also includes encountering the desires and feelings of others. In these cases, our own reactions are seldom neutral. The values of others frequently elicit feelings in us. Whether or not we have understood these feelings, our own response often includes feelings of sympathy with or reaction against what we feel they are feeling. In this way, the feelings of value that shape our lives end up becoming a curious intermingling of our own feelings and feelings evoked by our reactions to the feelings of others. Untangling these webs of feeling almost always plays a significant role in the resolving of conflicts.

Many of the decisions and actions of our lives are shaped by values operating on this first experiential level of feeling. What is interesting about this first level, however, is that most often, the feelings are about something, and they invite us to understand what they are about. They have a basis in past experiences, they tell a story about this past, and they direct our action towards future expectations rooted in this story. The problem is, on this first level, we often do not know what these stories are. In order to make these values more fully our own, we need to learn what they are about, and this takes us to a second group of operations of understanding where we reflect on our feelings, ask questions, and get insights into what they are about.

The second level involves understanding values. Here we get insights into what we are feeling, and we discover the narratives and social relations that are carried in these feelings. What we learn are narratives that situate us with respect to others within patterns of social relations. These narratives can take any number of forms: we are facing a challenge; we are appreciated by friends; we take pride in an achievement; we are solving a problem; we are helping another; we are running from danger; we are badgered by a bully; we are lost in a maze; we fail in a task; we have been abandoned. The narratives carry implicit ideas of how things ought or ought not to be, and they situate us in the present in relation to their trajectories. They establish expectations of future events that would happen were the value narrative to take its course, and they stamp these futures with an evaluative colouring that is rooted in past experience. Understanding values involves learning about the narratives that are carried by our feelings.

What makes value narratives so potent is the way they portray images of social relations and assign worth or value in terms of these patterns of social relations. Facing challenges frequently involves expectations about measuring up in the eyes of others, and the 'significant others' implicated in these images often involve family or peer groups. The idea of 'measuring up' conveyed in the feeling involves group belonging and fulfilling expectations. The appreciation of friends and pride in achievement are often meaningful in relation to family, neighbourhood, or workplace contexts. These contexts involve identities, roles, and tasks, and appreciation and pride are often linked to these. When we solve problems and help others, our sense of worth is often related both to the task and to the personal or professional relations involved. Danger is frequently more than merely physical danger. It often involves dangerous social contexts, and bullies are bullies precisely because of the harmful patterns of social relations they initiate and sustain. Finally, feelings of loss, failure, and abandonment are of lasting significance to us precisely because our lives are defined by a hunger and longing for the personal relations evoked by the narratives.

What we understand when we probe our feelings are narratives that situate us with respect to patterns of social relations. These narratives assign worth, disvalue, praise, or blame in relation to the expectations implied by these patterns. These normative or evaluative notions have the effect of directing our inclinations and actions along paths suggested by the narratives. Gaining insights into feelings can reveal a great deal about what we care about and why we care the way we do. It can help identify the cares and threats at work in conflicts and provide resources for resolving conflicts.

The third level is verifying values. Understanding values is not the final operation in the process of making them fully our own. The next group of learning operations along the way involves reflecting on what we have understood, scrutinizing our values and those of others, and asking questions for verification. In our relations with others, particularly relations involving conflicts, verifying values takes two different forms.

The first of these is empirical verification. It involves asking whether we have understood ourselves or others correctly. Are our insights correct? Is there something we have missed? Is there more involved in my own value narrative that includes my reactions to yours? Have I understood your values correctly? The goal here is not the evaluation of the values themselves; it is verifying whether our understanding of the narratives and normative social relations carried by the feelings is indeed correct. Have we understood the values correctly? This form of verification plays an important role in conflicts. Frequently conflicts involve misunderstandings about what parties truly care about. Distinguishing positions and interests involves probing beyond immediate problems in search of the underlying cares and concerns that are carried in feelings. Verification means checking to learn whether we have understood correctly – both ourselves and others.

The second meaning of verification is existential. Here we engage in the more personal, reflective process of evaluating and judging who we have become and what we have done. Are our values truly valuable? Or are they skewed, distorted, immature, or incomplete? Here, our goal is personal authenticity. Understanding the narratives and normative social relations carried in our feelings leads us to question whether they are mature or socially responsible. We reflect on our values, and ask: Are they reasonable? Are they adequate for adult social living? Do they reveal flaws that we need to address? Do we need to cultivate new habits and skills? Are we sufficiently attuned to social, political, gender, cultural, or environmental issues? Conflicts frequently challenge us to question our own values. But they also involve us in the critical judgment of the values of others. Indeed, conflicts frequently have their roots in these critical value judgments of other parties. Understanding the verification process calls us to reflect on how thorough, honest, or authentic we have been in our criticisms of our own values and those of others. It calls us to ask the same authenticity of others. Some models of conflict mediation focus on the potential for moral growth and development presented by these instances of verification.[18]

Understanding this second, existential sense of verification also invites us to ask whether value differences must necessarily lead to the dysfunctional social relations frequently involved in conflicts. Frequently, inverse insights can play a role in the verification process by reshaping our assumptions about how to act when we encounter value differences. Our own value narratives often lead us to expect actions that must follow necessarily once another's values are judged to be at odds with our own. Frequently, it is the necessity of these expectations that fuels conflict. Inverse insights invite us to question this necessity and shift to alternate lines of questioning. Here we ask how we might live differently with value differences. Verifying another's values, even when we judge them negatively, does not necessarily lock us into dysfunctional patterns of conflict. Quite frequently, judgments of their values become judgments of them as persons. Inverse insights invite us to de-link values from persons. They invite us to ask whether we might learn something new, perhaps even from them. In the following chapter, we explore how the two meanings of verification function in mediation, and how inverse insights play a role in living with value differences.

The fourth level is decision or acting on values. This is a fourth group of operations that carries us from understanding and verification into action. Here the operations build upon the results of the previous levels and take us into actions that implement the results of our deliberations and judgments. Here we ask about integrity: Are we willing to live by our values? Do we have the courage of our convictions? In mediation, this is the point where parties commit to action strategies and sign agreements. In adjudication processes, this is where parties either agree to comply with rulings or launch appeals.

What is interesting about this fourth stage is how it both completes the learning process and launches another cycle of learning through the four levels of the process. Decision results in action, and action yields consequences. These consequences, however, are often at odds with what we expected. In a sense, we can say that the consequences of decisions provide another round of evidence for verifying whether or not we have made good decisions. When we find we have not, we are called back to scrutinize our feelings and experiences, our direct and inverse insights, and our empirical and existential judgments that verify our understanding. In this way, we continue cycling through the four levels of the process throughout the learning of our lives. The consequences of our earlier understandings and decisions provide the experiential bases for later insights, judgments, and decisions.

Insight Theory also invites us to observe another way that decisions send us cycling back through the four-level learning process. This is the cycle of innovation. In this case, the order of the operations of the levels is reversed. Here decisions commit persons and groups to values that point out directions for action. On their own, however, the values do not specify how this direction is to be lived out. What follows are judgments of value that develop avenues of policy and indicate directions for carrying forward the project into diverse spheres of life and work. Insights then begin doing their creative work, innovating diverse ways in which these values can be concretized. Finally, action brings the circle of operations into the realm of concrete experience. This is the sort of thing that happens when organizations write mission statements and then develop innovative policies and organizational patterns for implementation. It is also what happens when parties in conflict come to a basic understanding and appreciation of each other's cares and concerns. They may or may not agree on fundamental values, but they make decisions on directions for living with the differences that remain. These decisions open the way for curiosity, creativity, and innovation in developing action strategies for living in new ways.

Concluding Remarks

It is time to bring this presentation of Insight Theory to a close. In the next chapter, we pick up on the main ideas of this chapter and apply Insight Theory to conflict and the mediation process. The key ideas that we work with in the next chapter are direct and inverse insights, verification, and feelings and values. Of central importance throughout the entire discussion, however, is the method of self-understanding that is foundational for Insight Theory. Understanding Lonergan's ideas requires more than simply reading articles and books. It requires cultivating the discipline of reflecting on our own experiences of insight, asking questions about these experiences, and getting insights into the personal moments of transformation that are central to the learning process. Above all, it requires curiosity and the cultivation of curiosity about ourselves, our operations of learning, and how they play a role in shaping our feelings and relations with others.

Our effort in the following chapters is to apply the fruits of these discoveries to the field of conflict. We believe that the discoveries of Insight Theory reveal fundamental challenges to the way we live with conflicts in democratic life. But we also argue that Insight Theory provides direction on how we can begin meeting these challenges. To move forward in these directions requires not simply a mechanical process of implementation, but a continued series of innovations. These innovations require the lifelong learning of insight, and this means a willingness to engage in the method of self-understanding that is fundamental to Insight Theory. Our hope is that this chapter and those that follow are intriguing enough to engage readers in taking up the invitation to self-discovery extended by Lonergan's work.

4 Insight Mediation: Applying Insight Theory to Mediation

The early years of conflict studies were charged with enthusiasm.[1] Centres were established, programs launched, and conflict services advertised for hire. In the air was an optimism that a professional practice based on solid scientific research could slowly but surely transform both domestic life and international affairs. Needless to say, events in the ensuing decades have tempered some of this optimism. Conflicts have proven complex and dangerous, and the field less developed than previously imagined.

Still, through all this realism, conflicts continue to be resolved. Even when outcomes cannot be called 'resolution,' intervention strategies open new avenues for living with differences. We are not always sure how this happens. Nor are we always sure how to make it happen again. But we do know that, sometimes, some interventions do help. Consequently, much of the original optimism about the role of conflict practitioners remains.

One of the experiences fuelling this optimism has been what practitioners call 'the magic of mediation.' It is a curious moment that has a feel to it: a change in the emotional dynamics of both interpersonal and group conflict interactions. Something shifts in the way individuals and groups relate. Those involved begin talking and working together in ways they could not have done before. The 'magic' happens often enough that mediators continue to talk about it and wonder about it. Insight Mediation, the approach used at Carleton University in Ottawa, was born out of this effort of talking and wondering.

Mediation has been taught and practised at Carleton since the early 1990s.[2] Much of the attention has focused on interpersonal and small-group conflicts in family, workplace, school, and community contexts.

First through the Mediation Centre, and now the Graduate Certificate in Conflict Resolution program and the Centre for Conflict Education and Research at Carleton University, mediators are trained to facilitate a process in which disputants work their own way towards understanding and agreement. Mediation at Carleton is a process of assisted negotiation where mediators have no power to impose outcomes. Rather, they do their work by facilitating parties as they work their way through the issues towards consensus. The process shares elements with most other interest-based models, but as will become evident in the following pages, it is also different. Similar to many early programs, Carleton's was not designed on the basis of a particular theoretical model. Like most mediators working in the 1970s and early 1980s, the program's founder, Cheryl Picard, was largely self-taught and developed her own style of practice. Her success as a mediator and trainer led to the establishment of programs for training and mentoring new mediators at Carleton.

With the publication of *The Promise of Mediation* by Robert Baruch Bush and Joseph Folger (1994) and *Narrative Mediation* by John Winslade and Gerald Monk (2000), mediators across North America launched into a vigorous activity of discussing and debating theoretical models. The Transformative and Narrative models each had their own distinctive styles, and they offered alternative explanations of how the mediation process worked and how intervention strategies functioned to promote outcomes. They were developed, in large measure, as alternatives to the interest-based approach that had dominated the field until then, particularly in business and legal contexts. This prompted mediators to begin situating themselves and their practices in relation to these approaches. They asked whether these new models captured and reflected what they did in mediation, and they sought to understand whether these models left things unsaid. This line of inquiry was pursued at Carleton, and it resulted in the Insight model of mediation being articulated in 2002.

A characteristic feature of interest-based approaches is a pragmatic focus on the problem. In this approach, mediators probe for underlying interests as a means for dealing with the issues related to the problem itself. Their concern is problem solving. Transformative and Narrative mediators take a different approach. Their focus is on relationships, so the lines of questioning of mediators in these models are different. They follow parties into diverse areas of personal and social experience. In Narrative approaches, culturally rooted meaning sets are explored intentionally, and conflicts are resolved through the construction of new stories. In Transformative approaches, mediators take a non-interventionist approach, and they follow parties into the topic areas of interest to them.

Carleton mediators and instructors feel an affinity with the Transformative and Narrative mediators' concern for relationships, and they use communication skills similar to ones used in these as well as interest-based approaches. Embedded in their approach, however, are lines of questioning that aim at different goals. Rather than focusing on problem solving, or constructing stories, or following parties' conversations moment-by-moment, Carleton mediators are taught to ask questions about what parties care about and how these cares are threatened. Instructors teach mediators to be curious about parties' stories and to ask questions about how past experiences shape present interpretations and expectations about the future. They engage parties in conversation to help them understand each other's meanings, particularly inaccurate meanings that exacerbate the conflict. Mediators help facilitate parties' learning about the conflict, each other's values, cares, and threats, and new possibilities for action. The goal of their questioning is to help parties achieve breakthroughs in perspectives and attitudes that shift relationships onto new ground. It aims at a deeper understanding of the concerns at stake and the cares that parties feel are threatened in the conflict.

One distinctive feature of Insight mediators' questioning is that it aims at evoking the parties' own questioning about what is truly important to them in the conflict and why. It aims at helping parties ask their own questions and get insights into what they care about and how this is threatened by the goals and pursuits of the other. Insight mediators' questions help parties look for ways that their cares and concerns can be met without threatening those of the other. Their questions are not directive, although mediators are intentionally curious and at times direct. Their curiosity aims at helping parties achieve a breakthrough that reshapes their perspective on the problem. Those of us involved in the Carleton program wanted to understand more about this distinctive line of questioning and what was going on in the breakthroughs that parties experienced when it proved successful.

To answer these questions, we turned to the Insight Theory of Bernard Lonergan and to a group of scholars researching Lonergan's work at Saint Paul University, Ottawa.[3] What we found was a wealth of ideas that help answer our questions. Insight Theory provides resources for understanding mediation as a process of transformative learning.[4] This learning involves careful attention to the data of the problem, but it carries the learner beyond the data to insight into relationships. The learning of insight transforms feelings, alters perspectives, and opens new possibilities for relationships. It evokes narratives, but grounds parties in a more accurate understanding of contexts and opportunities. Insight Theory presented tools for understanding the mediation practice at Carleton, and we believe it offers inroads into some of the more fundamental issues raised by the history of research on conflict.

Steps in the Insight Mediation Process

Like many mediation models, Insight Mediation involves a process in which mediators help parties tell their stories, explore underlying interests and concerns, and generate options for solving problems and reaching agreements.[5] The process involves five steps that generally unfold in a non-linear pattern, with parties moving back and forth among the steps until they feel comfortable making decisions together. Because Insight Mediation is based on a relational philosophy, it is less pragmatic in its efforts towards finding resolution and more focused on ensuring that parties have the opportunity to engage in fair and fruitful conversations.

The Five Steps of Insight Mediation
1. *Attend to Process*
2. *Broaden Understanding*
3. *Deepen Insights*
4. *Explore Possibilities*
5. *Make Decisions*

In step one, *Attend to Process*, the goal is for the mediator and parties to arrive at a shared understanding of the process and protocols to be used in the mediation session, and for parties to agree to proceed on the basis of this understanding. Typical mediation protocols often involve listening while the other is speaking, agreeing not to interrupt, expressing one's own experience of the problem, avoiding blame and accusation, being open and forthcoming with information, and deciding if matters need to be kept confidential. Parties also agree on a time limit for the session, and they establish whether they have the authority to make decisions on their own or whether ratification by others is required. Building rapport in this step is important for Insight mediators, and they do this by demonstrating their ability to listen and respond to parties fairly and non-judgmentally.

In step two, *Broaden Understanding*, mediators invite parties to state what they have come to talk to each other about and what they hope will be different if they are able to have that conversation. Beginning mediation by stating hopes about a productive conversation, rather than re-articulating demands, has the effect of setting the discussion on a positive footing and encouraging parties to begin the hard work involved in mediation. More often than not, parties have similar hopes: a better working relationship, a more peaceful home life, happier times together, connecting in new ways, or simply getting on with their lives. In this step, mediators seek to broaden knowledge about the conflict by discovering how the parties experience the conflict as threatening something important to them.

Step three, *Deepen Insights*, involves identifying and probing more deeply into feelings to understand the values, cares, and threats that lie behind the issues in the dispute. Here is where the important learning occurs. In this step, mediators are particularly empathetic and non-judgmental, and they draw heavily upon curiosity, skills of reflective listening, and strategies of deepening, to evoke the parties' own questioning about what lies below the surface of the conflict. They know that feelings of threat are often linked to past experiences, present behaviours, and expectations about the future, and their interventions are aimed at helping parties gain insights into how these are at work in the conflict. When parties begin understanding the reasons behind the actions of others, they often discover these actions to be rooted in things that matter deeply, and not simply ill will. Based on their experiences and the insights provided by the theoretical model, mediators know that gaining this understanding is often difficult. Yet they remain confident that understanding and appreciating what matters to each party can reconfigure their meaning sets and open avenues for collaboration. Mediators know that parties can care about what others care about when doing so does not threaten what matters to them. This, we believe, is an important dimension of the relational philosophy at the heart of Insight Mediation.

The fourth step in the Insight Mediation process, *Explore Possibilities*, often begins quite naturally and easily once parties gain insights into the values and cares behind actions, overcome barriers imposed by feelings of threat, and come to realize that both sets of cares can coexist.

The insights of step three provide new information, clarify misinformation, reformulate parties' meaning sets, and pave the way for collaboration. The challenge, then, is to work together to implement the cares and reduce the threats, and frequently parties take their own initiative to move into the exploration step. At this point, the mediator's work shifts to one of facilitating this exploration and helping parties discover options that resolve the issues that brought them to mediation.

Finally, in step five, *Make Decisions*, parties agree on directions for action, and they bring the process to conclusion. At every step along the way, the process is consensual, and parties hold the power to move the process in whichever direction they need to feel comfortable with outcomes. While Insight mediators are intentional in their efforts to enhance communication between parties, they are not directive about outcomes. Their aim is to help parties gain their own insights. They do this by respecting each party's need for a safe place for exploring what matters to them and to the other. What follows is a sense of empowerment and an ability to make collaborative decisions.

Clearly, then, a good deal of the Insight mediator's time is spent working in step three. Parties have difficulty resolving conflicts as long as they remain focused on habitual ways of understanding the problem and each other. To move towards satisfactory outcomes requires exploring new understandings, and so after the brief statements of step two, Insight mediators help parties enter this exploration process in step three. They also know that parties can explore problem-solving options with relative ease once they overcome barriers presented by feelings of threat. Steps four and five are seldom charged with the emotional intensity of earlier steps because threats have been removed or brought in the open for discussion, and parties often move through the remaining steps with little help from the mediator. Conversely, when parties move prematurely to steps four and five, they encounter difficulties that bring them back to stage three, to the values, cares, and threats that underlie the conflict. Consequently, the focus of the process in Insight Mediation is step three, *Deepen Insights*. This is the step where the 'magic' most often happens.

Principles of Insight Mediation

As researchers seeking to understand and explain the distinctive features of Insight Mediation, we were particularly curious about the principles that give rise to Insight mediator strategies.[6] How are parties as persons understood, and how is the role of mediators understood? What are mediators looking to do when they probe for underlying cares and threats? How do these cares and threats function to create and sustain conflicts? What happens when parties make breakthroughs that open new avenues for resolution? What is the 'magic' really about? Insight Theory provided resources for answering these questions. Based on our findings, we formulated the following principles to help guide Insight mediators in their work. You will notice that these principles reflect a social theory of the human person and a relational philosophy of conflict.

The first principle of Insight Mediation is about the social nature of persons. Insight mediators understand that we are individual persons and we are actors in our relations with others: we are agents of meaning, we perform operations of meaning, and these operations shape our interactions with the world. At the same time, we are also social. Our operations of meaning take us out of ourselves into engagement with others, and this engagement shapes our actions and our identity as persons. Our lives are lived in relationships with others, we share things with others, and we seek to understand each other. We are shaped by our traditions, we live in communities, and we seek to understand ourselves and others in relation to these traditions and communities.

Second, as Insight mediators we know that peoples' actions are not purely self-interested. Actions arise from deeply held convictions about how people should engage with others in the world. These convictions are values that shape how we care about others and also how we feel threatened in the world. They include things we are interested in and things we need for our lives, relationships, and communities. Even when we have difficulty articulating our values, they remain at work guiding our actions, directing our cares and feelings of threat, shaping our sense of identity, and situating us in relation to others. Values manifest themselves in feelings: the stronger the value, the more intense the feeling. Insight mediators believe that understanding our actions involves acknowledging our feelings and gaining insight into the values, cares, and threats that lie behind them.

The third principle concerns the way values, cares, and threats work in conflicts. Insight mediators understand that conflicts arise when we believe that our cares are threatened by those of others. Because conflicts involve values, we experience threats to our values as threats to ourselves as persons. Consequently, dealing with conflicts requires not only acknowledging feelings and naming values, it also requires learning – understanding values, how they work, how they are related to the values of others, how they are threatened, how they pose a threat to others, and how these feelings and values shape our sense of self and our relations with others.

Fourth, Insight mediators know that understanding values can change how we experience conflict, and this can play a significant role in resolving conflict. Understanding involves insight, and when insights get to the root of things, they are not merely intellectual; they are also affective. They shift the way we think and feel about values, both our own and those of others. This emotional shift shapes participants' horizons, and can shift the conflict situation from impasse to openness, opening doors to collaborative problem solving.

These four principles establish an overall shape and texture to the Insight Mediation process and a distinct way of understanding conflict. As we interact with others, our actions are informed by values, and our reactions to them are directed not only towards the outward form of their actions, but also towards the meaning of their actions and the values we feel are behind them. Most important, we react to the way other people's values pose a threat to our own. Values are expressed in both words and actions, and interpreting values gets us into the complex webs of meaning that inform both our own lives and those of others. Because values matter to us, we react strongly when we encounter values that seem to threaten our own. The conflicts that result get doubly complicated by hidden values – values we did not know we had; values that often come from more remote regions of our own past.

Insight mediators help disputants through these tangled webs of meanings, cares, and threats. They journey with parties and help them learn ways they can travel together. They do this work by helping them work through real and perceived threats. Their principal tool is curiosity, and their questions aim to evoke curiosity in the parties, curiosity about their own values as well as those of others. They probe to help parties discover the frameworks or 'horizons' of meaning that help explain why things matter to them.[7] Participants bring their own past histories to conflicts, and these pasts set frameworks for the meaning of actions in the present. Past events have a way of projecting sets of expectations about the future, and these expectations play a role in shaping parties' actions towards each other. Insight mediators help parties become curious and gain insights about these frameworks. Learning how past images and expectations about the future are linked to present events is the work of insight, and insight can open avenues for collaboration.

The case of Danny and Teresa provides an illustration of some of these principles of Insight Mediation in action.[8] In this workplace-based conflict, Danny resisted cooperating with Teresa in her efforts to modernize the documents section of the library because, in the past, ideas such as hers resulted in lay-offs and work displacements. Danny and his colleagues imagined this was going to happen again, and so her work assignment posed a threat to them. They liked their jobs and believed things were working well enough. Given their negative experiences of past organizational restructuring, they anticipated something similar happening again in the future, and so Danny and his teammates refused to cooperate with Teresa.

Teresa, on the other hand, had consulted with staff, and found the majority in favour of the proposed changes. She was puzzled and frustrated because Danny's group refused to engage in the discussions. She needed the cooperation of everyone for her implementation plan to be successful. Teresa's past included a similar experience in a different workplace where she concluded that the opponents to change in that situation were simply too old or too lazy. She came to fear that this was the case again and that Danny's group would get in the way of her being able to do her job well.

The present situation evoked in both Danny and Teresa past narratives that projected fears about future outcomes. In both cases, their actions in the conflict were rooted in real values, but narratives from past experience gave rise to expectations of threat to these values. As the mediation took its course, both parties gained insight into the cares and feelings of threat at work in the conflict and how these structured the conflict relationship. This learning opened opportunities for exploring ways that values could be respected and threats avoided, and they had the effect of shifting the emotional dynamics of the conflict and restructuring the parties' relationship.

Feelings as Carriers of Values, Cares, and Threats

Conflict practitioners know that the issues that command the focus of parties' attention seldom tell the whole story of what conflicts are about. Getting to the place where resolution can begin requires probing beyond the presenting problem in search of deeper cares and threats. When Insight mediators probe for cares and threats, one of the important areas they explore is feelings. All too often, the feelings fuelling conflict are intense and negative, and they involve hurt, fear, disappointment, and loss. While parties focus their attention on their positions towards issues, the tenacity with which they hold to their positions seldom can be explained in terms of the issues or events of the situation alone. What drives their attachment to their positions are feelings and the cares and threats that are carried in these feelings.

Insight Theory offers a framework for understanding how feelings, cares, and threats function in conflict.[9] Insight mediators use the language of cares and threats in mediation and Lonergan's philosophy presents a theory of feelings and values that helps explain how cares and threats function to dynamize conflict. Feelings carry deeper values, but they often do this work without our reflective awareness or understanding. Feelings arise from earlier life experiences, and they carry implicit narratives that are rooted in these experiences. These narratives carry judgments and expectations about what is important, how things should be, what should happen were life to follow its proper course. They establish patterns of social organization that we think should be operative in life. They direct our cares and fears, they shape our identities, they exert an influence on our decisions and actions, and they set the framework for our evaluations of others. They do this work on the level of feeling, and this helps explain why values often are unrecognized or ignored in conflicts. Parties in conflict tend to 'feel' more than 'think,' and they seldom reflect upon their own values, let alone the values of others. In many cases, values are never articulated. We cannot recall the earlier life experiences that gave rise to the feelings, nor do we understand the values that the feelings are about. The feelings remain vibrant and alive while the values behind them remain obscure.

Because the values carried in feelings are so often obscure, we often do not know why we feel so strongly about issues. We simply do. This adds considerable complexity to conflicts. When dynamized by value-laden feelings, conflicts are rarely about what we are arguing about. The values remain below the surface. The trouble is, we do not know this, so we go on hammering away at the issues and at each other. Insight mediators are trained to help parties explore these feelings and gain insights that give voice to the underlying values. Feelings evoke Insight mediators' curiosity about 'why things matter.'

Insight Theory provides some interesting ideas about values that guide mediators in their work. The first involves the narrative structure of values. Often we think of values as individual actions or goals, for example, truth telling or personal security. However, these are only pieces of a larger whole, and understanding this larger whole requires observing how values do their work in our lives. Values orient us, they direct our interest and attention, they shape our expectations of future events, and they guide our decisions and actions. They do this because they have a narrative structure to them. Values have their origins in past events, but their influence in our lives is not limited to interpreting these pasts. These pasts situate us within particular interpretations of the present that lead to specific expectations about the future. Our notions of value are rooted in the vectors or directions expressed by these past-present-future trajectories. Something is important to us in the present because past experiences have taught us about actions that have positive or negative consequences for the future. Whether we learn these narratives from our own experiences, or whether they are passed on to us through families, cultures, or traditions, these narratives do their work by projecting future expectations of hope, fear, anticipation, or dread. We observe these narratives at work when women and men come to Canada from war-torn countries where they have experienced the military and police as enemies not to be trusted. Their past narratives of fear and mistrust are projected onto Canadian police and military personnel, and these expectations can give rise to considerable difficulty relating to women and men in uniform.

Related to this narrative structure are the expectations about social relations that are carried in these value narratives. Value narratives not only situate us with respect to our own pasts and futures, but they also situate us within patterns of social relations with others. They project images about how to work within these social relations and what we ought and ought not to do to help social life function at its best. Our narratives assign worth or value to actions in relation to these social patterns. We carry with us hosts of expectations about how families, workplaces, conversations, schools, consumer transactions, neighbourhood relations, and political events function and ought to function. These expectations form part of our value narratives, and they have the effect of shaping our evaluations of others. We observe clashes in these social expectations when the cultural norms and values of second generation Canadians come in conflict with parents or grandparents not born and raised in Canada.

Insight mediators ask questions that probe the experiences of parties and help them gain insights into the value narratives carried in feelings. Values often do their work shaping interpretations and evaluations without the conscious awareness of parties themselves. To learn why they interpret events and react to others as they do, parties need to get insights into their own value narratives as well as those of other parties. This requires considerable curiosity and exploration. Exploring values involves mediators discovering why things matter and what parties expect to happen were events to take their course. This involves helping them understand the patterns of social relations implied in the narratives. Discovering values also involves mediators affirming parties and encouraging them to own and express their cares and concerns. It can involve probing past events and evoking experiences, not simply from their interactions with other parties in the conflict, but also from earlier events of their own past. Value narratives often have their origins in earlier life experiences, and coming to understand what matters in conflicts can involve retrieving events associated with these earlier life experiences. The mediator's goal here is not to act as therapist, but simply to make sense of convictions and actions that otherwise appear senseless.

When mediators help parties discover and give voice to values, some of the frustration and anxiety of conflict eases. This is particularly the case when values are acknowledged by the other party. A sense of clarity begins to emerge, and parties start to feel more confident. Understanding values allows parties to recognize the reasons behind the conflict and to affirm something legitimate about their stance. It also provides tools for exploring alternative routes through the issues. As confidence grows, so too does curiosity. Insight mediators facilitate parties' curiosity about what matters to others and how their cares and concerns can be met in alternative ways. It is this shift that brings about the 'magic' of mediation.

Another feature from Insight Theory concerns the way value narratives do their work by functioning as types or models. When we encounter situations in life, we interpret these situations in the light of past experiences, and our inventory of value narratives provides us with a tool kit of types that we use for interpreting present experiences. If, for instance, we are in a situation that evokes a manipulation narrative, we begin looking for signs of manipulation in the actions of others. We begin expecting manipulation with all of its negative consequences. This launches us into a program of action for defending ourselves against these negative futures. Many experiences are similar to other experiences in life, and learning to handle new experiences involves identifying types or models that prescribe ways of acting in similar situations. Value narratives contain implicit markers that signal to us when we are in situations where past narratives are relevant for interpreting present events. When this happens, the value narratives do their work by projecting sets of future anticipations and expectations. These future expectations carried by value narratives set the standards for evaluating our own actions and those of others.

Insight mediators explore parties' feelings and experiences so they can help determine whether the value narratives are applicable to the present conflict. Because value narratives function as types, they are easily invoked by current experiences, but often do not provide reliable or complete reference frames for interpreting present events. For example, a mediator observes a party's feelings of fear and begins asking what is worrisome. What emerges is a narrative in which a previous coworker's display of expertise and skill resulted in her losing a chance for promotion. She felt that the other's expertise resulted in harm to her. Probing the feeling of fear reveals a value – protection from harm. But the narrative's particular configuration of values of expertise and protection from harm leads her to interpret the other party's expertise and skill as necessarily a threat. Insight mediators help parties discern the connection between the past feelings and present experiences. Very often this involves learning that the current conflict need not unfold as a replay of the earlier experience. The present can take its own course, and in this example, the party can exercise his expertise and skill without posing the threat evoked by the narrative.

Value narratives tend to bring conviction and certainty with them, and this certainty has its roots in the stories and images from previous life events. Often this certainty is not required, either by the values themselves or by present contexts. Once values are understood and affirmed, we can be innovative and creative in living them out. Until underlying values are discerned, parties tend to keep an iron grip on positions. The narratives carried by their feelings present the negative consequences as a virtual certainty. When Insight mediators help parties learn about their value narratives, they provide the means for moving out of the certainty associated with threat. They help make uncertain what before was certain. What follows is curiosity, flexibility, and creativity. Even when values proscribe specific measures, they often leave room for diverse ways of achieving their specific objectives. Understanding and affirming values can open paths for parties to explore novel options for their realization.

Contrary to popular opinion, affirming values does not lock parties in conflict. In fact, quite often the opposite is the case. When Insight mediators help parties understand and affirm values operative in feelings, it becomes easier for the parties to explore alternative options for their achievement. Once they discover and affirm their underlying values, they can de-link these values from feelings of certain threat and from the positions that originally locked them in conflict. This de-linking can open up new lines of curiosity and questioning.[10]

Sometimes values actually are in conflict and perceived threats are real. What is important, in these cases, is understanding the boundaries of the conflicts and threats. This is what can be achieved through the insights that understand the values operative in parties' feelings. Even when values conflict, the range of options permitted by the values need not require the intense conflictual engagement that previously defined the parties' interactions. Once the values are discovered and affirmed, participants can explore options for living separately or charting courses of action that do not involve the recurrent clash of values. Here, the creativity mobilized is around action strategies for living with value differences. To mobilize this creativity requires the prior process of understanding and affirming values. Without the security provided by this learning, parties' feelings of threat will not allow them to engage the curiosity necessary for moving beyond postures of self-defence.

There is one more feature of importance from Insight Theory, related to the existential character of value judgments, that plays an important role in Insight Mediation. Our values shape our identity. They make a claim on our actions because they make a claim on us as persons. Values are implicated in our sense of self-worth, and they shape the way we interpret others. When others perform actions that threaten to damage the social relations carried in our value narratives, we not only experience our values as threatened, but we also experience ourselves as threatened. There is a profound linkage between the values carried in feelings and our feelings of self. This also goes for our interpretations of others. When their actions threaten our values, we experience *them* as a threat. We move seamlessly from evaluation of actions to the evaluation of persons – both ourselves and others. When our evaluations of people form the basis for our response to them, then actions directed against their values become an attack on them as persons. They feel this personal attack, and often respond in ways that escalate the conflict. Because these personal evaluations are so often carried by the narratives that remain concealed in feelings, we remain unaware of how this process has transpired.

Insight mediators help parties avoid the threats implied by accusation, criticism, and blame by helping parties reformulate their cares and responses in ways that distinguish between actions and persons, and by helping them find alternative ways of expressing cares and concerns. At the core of this work is helping parties discover that we can, indeed, distinguish between what we do and who we are as persons. Mediators can also help parties distinguish between another's actions and the emotional responses evoked by these actions, and this has the effect of giving parties some control over their own responses. Your actions may evoke a response of anger in me. But this does not require that I criticize or blame you. I can de-link your actions from you as a person and focus the conversation, not on blame, but on specific values and actions. I can also de-link your actions from my own response. This has the effect of re-interpreting your actions, not as an attack on me, but as a response to my actions. Finally, it allows me to own my own response, thus giving me some control over the conflict. All of these involve insights that generate new learning and open parties to new ways of acting and relating in conflicts. Insight Theory's understanding of the relationship between values and identity helps explain the mediator strategies that guide parties through this work.

The Strategy of Linking: Gaining Direct Insights into Cares and Threats

An important strategy of Insight mediators is 'linking.' While parties come into the mediation focused on their positions, mediators pay close attention to their stories, listening for clues to the deeper values underlying each party's involvement in the dispute, the things that really matter to them. They pay particular attention to discrepancies among various parties' descriptions of events, observations, assumptions, and expectations, discrepancies that provide clues to the particular cares and concerns of each. They listen for information that helps link current feelings to past events. Their questions aim at evoking parties' curiosity about these linkages. Does the present conflict suggest something similar that happened in the past? What is important about this past for the present? How is it linked to the party's actions in the present? How is it linked to his or her expectations about the future? While these questions are prompted, initially, by the mediator's own curiosity, they are aimed at evoking the party's curiosity about the deeper value narratives at work in the conflict.

One of the important features of value narratives is the way they project expectations about the future. When a party's involvement in conflict is dynamized by a particular value narrative, then that story's outcome will provide the formula for his expectations about the future of the present conflict. If I am proven wrong in a conflict, my story is that I will be shown to be a failure and a fool, and I will be rejected by friends and loved ones. Mediators ask questions to help identify and draw out these implicit expectations. What do you think will happen if the others get what they want? What do you think will happen if you do not get what you want? Quite often, the threats that dynamize a party's involvement in conflicts are contained in these expectations. But because the value narratives are carried in feelings, they often remain hidden and cannot be dealt with until they become externalized and understood. Connecting issues to underlying values, past narratives, and anticipated outcomes is the goal of linking.

Insight mediators believe that conflicts arise for good reasons. Conflicts are often handled badly, and at times they result in suffering, violence, and terrible evil. But whether or not they are handled well, they arise for good reasons. This is because conflicts are rooted in values. Conflicts arise because actions are grounded in values, and something in these values poses a challenge or a threat to the values of others. The same holds true for the values of others and the way they challenge or threaten our own. This way of understanding conflict lends a distinctive shape and texture to Insight Mediation. It means that conflicts are important for relationships because they signal that something significant requires attention. Conflict invites us to probe deeper to learn more about the underlying issues that need to be sorted out for the good of relationships, and this learning happens through linking.

The path that Insight mediators take in doing this work is the path of insight. The role of mediators is not to make judgments about parties' values; it is to help them gain insights into these values – both their own and those of others. It is to help them understand and appreciate what matters to themselves and others so they can move past the blockages posed by feelings of threat. Parties have difficulty charting courses of cooperative action when they feel their values are threatened by others. Often these threats are real. Insight mediators do not suppose that conflicts are simply the result of mistaken interpretations. What they do assume is that value conflicts, whether presumed or real, do not need to pronounce the last word on relationships. Values can be lived out in diverse ways, and learning about what matters to parties can open avenues for averting actions that threaten what matters to others. Furthermore, Insight mediators assume that there is something important in the cares and concerns of parties that needs to be understood and appreciated by all. Facilitating this understanding and appreciation has the effect of releasing the curiosity and creativity required for charting future paths in relationships.

The goal of Insight mediators is not to diagnose conflicts and pronounce solutions. Rather, their role is facilitating parties' own insights. They do this by engaging lines of questioning that seek to evoke parties' curiosity. Insights only arise as a response to questions, and this means that for parties to get insights, they themselves must become curious; they must be the ones asking questions. Insight mediators help parties move into this attitude of wonder and curiosity about what matters to themselves and others. This requires a complex and dynamic interaction between the mediator's own questioning and the parties' attitudes towards each other. When parties feel threatened, they become preoccupied with defence, and one of the first things to shut down is curiosity. In order for mediators to help parties regain this curiosity, they need to determine what is going on in the conflict, and this requires probing for the source of feelings of threat. Their own questioning aims at locating this source, but their goal is not satisfying the mediator's curiosity; it is locating the experiences and insights that evoke the interest and curiosity of the parties themselves. Their questioning throughout the mediation is in service of the parties' own questioning and learning. Insight mediator strategies have a focus and intentionality, but it is an intentionality that is responsive to and in service of the parties' own lines of interest and curiosity. Insight Mediation calls this *responsive intentionality.*

Insight mediators do their work by listening: they are interested; they are curious; they ask questions; they wonder; they probe for concerns, meanings, motives, cares, and needs. They notice what the parties say, and they listen for discrepancies between words and actions. They follow up on these discrepancies in search of underlying cares and threats that parties may not have formulated for themselves. They follow hunches; they verify possibilities; they acknowledge parties' feelings and insights; and they validate cares and concerns. They paraphrase to ensure they have understood correctly and to allow parties to hear, perhaps for the first time, what really matters to them and others. They reassure parties that they are listening and that what they say matters. They search for ways that parties can save face and negotiate out of 'corners' they may have backed into.

One of the important tools that mediators use in pursuing the goals of linking is *deepening*. Deepening work is done to learn more about a conflict narrative behind an issue that has surfaced as important to a party. After recognizing that something matters, the mediator becomes curious, and to understand better, probes for further insight. She begins with a statement that shows she has heard that something is important, and then follows up with an open question that expresses curiosity about the experience. The following example helps clarify how deepening works to help parties achieve the goals of linking.

In a mediation session, a father states: 'It upsets me that my daughter does not want a church wedding, so much so that we can't even talk about it without one or both of us becoming angry.' The mediator responds by reflecting his feeling: 'This is clearly a difficult and disappointing experience for you.' She then asks: 'What is so disappointing that you now find it difficult to talk with your daughter without becoming angry?' The mediator has acknowledged the feeling and named what is important in the feeling: they can no longer talk about the wedding in a fruitful way. Then in a follow-up, she asks a further question that deepens the discussion of the issue: 'When you find yourself disagreeing with your daughter on issues related to the wedding, what goes through your mind?' The father responds by stating: 'Actually, it makes me wonder if we will ever get back to enjoying the close relationship we've always had.' In response, the mediator then names the underlying value of maintaining a close relationship with his daughter: 'You clearly value your relationship with your daughter.' What begins to emerge through deepening is not only the value of the church wedding, but also the value of a close relationship that fosters communication and understanding between father and daughter.

The mediator next asks the father: 'What would be lost or sacrificed if your daughter does not have a church wedding?' The strategy here is to deepen by linking. The mediator is probing for the underlying value narrative with its projection of future expectations. Her interest is in identifying how something important (the value) is threatened by this projection of future expectations.

What emerges in the father's response is an expectation about his daughter 'living in sin,' and his own concerns about facing the priest and other members of his congregation were she to proceed with a small wedding on the beach. What also emerges is the admission that he has not been able to explain this to her. Of value to him is having this conversation with her about what her wedding means to him and how much it matters to him that her wedding be 'perfect.' The mediator then asks the father and daughter if this might be the time for them to have that conversation. After they agree, she invites the father to start by saying: 'Given that this is a conversation important to both of you, perhaps you could begin by elaborating on your fears, on what is important to you about your daughter's wedding, and what would be lost for you if she were to marry on the beach.' Once again, the mediator has reflected the feeling, and then proceeded to explore deeper by asking a question that relates to the father's response to a previous question.

In this instance, deepening is aimed at surfacing the value narrative with its implied expectations of future consequences. It is also aimed at *finishing*, a tool Insight mediators use to ensure that parties have said all they need to say about a topic they have had difficulty discussing in the past. Deepening and finishing allow parties to have conversations about things that matter to them in environments where they feel safe enough to explore values and have them affirmed and appreciated by mediators and other parties. It is this understanding, affirmation, and appreciation that often enables parties to explore alternate ways of meeting their respective values and goals. Gaining insights into these values is central to the strategy of linking.

The Strategy of De-Linking: Overcome Barriers through Inverse Insight

A second important strategy of Insight mediators is 'de-linking.' Here, mediators help parties gain inverse insights that de-link expectations of threat and open avenues for alternative ways of acting together. Insight Theory offers a rich and novel understanding of the role of inverse insights in the learning process, and mediators and teachers at Carleton University have found this concept helpful in explaining what they do. To begin this discussion of de-linking, we recall some of the distinctive features of direct and inverse insights from our presentation of Insight Theory in the previous chapter.

Insights do not fall from the sky, nor are they deliberate or fanciful constructions of the mind. They arise as a response to specific questions and from an engagement in a specific field of experiences. Questions have a focus and a direction to them, they ask about specific things, and they have their own internal criteria or requirements that point our inquiry in a particular direction. The questions ask about the experiential data, and the data have their own inner criteria or requirements.

When we get insights that make sense of our experiences, it is because the insights fulfil both sets of requirements. Three things come together when understanding proves reliable: 1) a particular body of data of our experiences; 2) a question that aims at a specific meaning or intelligibility in this particular body of experiences; and 3) the insight that grasps this meaning or intelligibility and fulfils the demands of both the question and the experiences.

For example, when we ask another person why he or she has been lying to us, the question presupposes that the person has told a lie, and it asks for reasons behind this action. The question aims at something quite specific. The question is also about a particular event, and the experiential features of the event exhibit characteristics that are also quite specific. When defending ourselves against criticism, we often cite these specific features to support our actions. In our example, if we learn by way of an insight that the person is trying to protect someone else from harm, and if we verify that experience indeed bears this out, then we rest satisfied with this meaning and act accordingly. This is what we mean when we say that an insight meets the demands of both the question and the experience.

The point to all of this is that for learning to prove reliable, we need all three components to come together and line up. This has important implications for the inquiry process, for the questions we ask when searching for insights. To get insights that sustain the test of verification, we need to find questions that lead us in directions that relate adequately to the particular experiences we seek to understand. The questions need to line up with the experiences. How often do we find ourselves exasperated, exhausted from trying to understand something, only to stumble on a seemingly unrelated issue that shifts us out of our line of questioning. We discover our prior line of questioning to be a dead-end street. We were barking up the wrong tree. We may hit on the more fruitful approach immediately, or we may need more time to explore further to discover the better line of questioning. What we get in these moments are inverse insights. They are not the insights that answer our questions. What they do is discover something inadequate in the questions we have been asking.

What inverse insights discover is that the expected meaning or intelligibility implied in the questioning is not present in the particular body of experience. Questions bring specific expectations to our experiences. They orient us in particular directions because they lead us to expect certain things in the experiences. Inverse insights disengage us from these expectations, and they open up our learning to new lines of questioning that explore alternative pathways.

To return to our example of the lie, a common way of asking about a person's lying is to ask why they have been manipulating us. The question here includes a specific expectation about what we will find in examining the data – manipulation. Often, however, this expectation is never formulated explicitly. It is frequently carried in the tone of voice or the body language. Yet, it remains operative guiding the inquiry process, sending us in search of evidence and motives for manipulation. What the inverse insight discovers is that these expectations are misplaced. In our example, this occurs when we discover evidence of something else at play in the situation: the lie is protecting someone from harm. What gives way is our expectation of manipulation, and our questioning opens up to allow a wider range of expected possibilities. We might get the new insights about the full reasons for the lie immediately, or it may take us some further time. What is important is that we have moved out of the previous focus on manipulation and are now free to pursue a wider range of questioning. This is achieved by the inverse insight.

Inverse insights are important for mediators because they help parties de-link from an attachment to misplaced expectations. This is particularly important when parties' expectations include the anticipation of harm or threat resulting from how they interpret the cares and concerns of others. While conflicts invariably have some basis in reality, disputants' feelings and interpretations can also involve distortions or misinterpretations. Sometimes parties' interpretations of others' values are distorted by value narratives from their own past. At other times, parties may be correct about others' values, but incorrect about whether pursuing these values must necessarily result in the expected threat. At work in both these scenarios are expectations of threat that are, in one way or another, misguided. These expectations exert considerable influence over parties' interactions in the conflict. Inverse insights de-link parties from these misplaced expectations and liberate curiosity to explore alternate ways of relating.

There are times when mediators discover that parties' expectations of threat are valid. Spouses may be abusive and partners' addictions may be real. In such cases, mediators help parties gain inverse insights into the necessity or inevitability of continued abuse or victimization. To be sure, such interventions often require referral to counsellors, police, or support agencies to help parties move on to alternate life paths. What is important for our purposes is the role of inverse insights in this process of moving on. Conflicts, even when they involve violence and abuse, often draw parties into distorted expectations about the necessity or inevitability of their situation. These expectations play a key role in locking them into dysfunctional patterns of relating. Parties feel there is no way out. The road to resolution and healing requires challenging these expectations of inevitability. Achieving the inverse insights necessary for getting out of these patterns can be extremely difficult.

Oftentimes the strategy of de-linking is straightforward. Take, for example, a divorcing parent who is convinced that his spouse is deliberately trying to make him look foolish or incompetent. They live apart and share custody of the children. She attempts to engage him in a conversation about parenting, but he refuses. As the mediator probes the reasons behind his refusal, she discovers him asking his spouse: 'Why do you continue to humiliate me?' What becomes apparent is that his resistance to the parenting conversation is not a resistance to the parenting conversation per se; it is a resistance to the expected threat of humiliation. As the mediator probes deeper into these expectations, she helps him discover the value narrative behind his fears and helps de-link the fear of humiliation from the parenting conversation. It is the necessary connection between the parenting conversation and the expectation of humiliation that the inverse insight pronounces misplaced.

In another example, a long-time employee is assigned a new boss who is young and eager to implement changes in the organization. She responds with resistance, interpreting the boss's desire for change as a gesture of contempt towards her previous achievements. She is incapable of showing interest in the boss's program and conflict results. As the mediator probes the reasons for the employee's resistance, he discovers a value narrative from the past that has shaped her interpretation of the present. In the narrative, authority figures did indeed display contempt for her achievements, and change was unjustly directed as a criticism of past performance. What he also probes are the reasons behind the new boss's programs and what emerges is an articulation of his respect for her contributions to the organization. The value narrative from the past does not apply to the present situation. Her response is surprise and curiosity. 'So what, then, are you trying to achieve?' When the mediator helps the party de-link interpretations of the present from the threat implied by past value narratives, her curiosity about her boss's program is liberated in new ways.

A third example concerns an environmental dispute. After days of discussion, an environmental group finally accepts that a developer is serious about committing considerable funds to ensure that wetlands are protected. At play in their interpretation of the developer was a value narrative arising from previous experiences. Their expectation was that he was focused only on short-term profits and had no concern for the environment. As the mediator probes these expectations, she is able to de-link their attitude towards the developer from the certainty arising from the past narrative. What held them in conflict was their conviction that this past must replay itself inevitably in the present. Once they were able to de-link from this sense of certainty, they began asking new questions that explored strategies for ensuring that promises would be kept and wetlands protected.

What is important about the strategy of de-linking is how it shifts parties from certainty to uncertainty in their interpretations of others' actions and intentions in the conflict. This shift is a key element in learning. Insight Mediation assumes that an important force holding parties in conflict is the attitude of certainty, particularly certainty around expectations of harm or threat. It is the necessity of this expectation that helps explain why conflicts seem intractable. Philip and Réjean want to talk through important issues of their relationship, but Philip associates talking, particularly talking about personal feelings, with past experiences of hurt and grief. When the mediator is successful in helping them past this blockage, it is the necessity or intractability of these associations that gets de-linked in the inverse insight. The curiosity required for probing relationship issues needs a prior uncertainty: an uncertainty about the outcome of this conversation. As long as we remain certain that a course of action contains a threat, we cannot give ourselves over to authentic questioning. To explore requires admitting we do not already know. Uncertainty about answers is the condition of possibility for genuine questioning. De-linking aims at establishing this posture of uncertainty that is needed for parties to be genuinely curious about what matters to them in the conflict.

The Strategy of Verification: Ensuring Insights are Correct

There is one final strategy that plays an important role in Insight Mediation. This is the strategy of verification. Recall, from the previous chapter, that verification does not ask about further insights; it asks whether a given insight is indeed an accurate response to a question, and whether it makes sense of a given body of experiential data. Verification aims at assuring that the three components – insights, questions, and experiences – come together and line up in the learning process. Verification pronounces that this is, indeed, the case. What is important for mediators is not the existential process of making judgments about values; it is the empirical process of verifying whether the mediator's or the parties' insights about what matters has not been misunderstood. Insight mediators' do this work of verification by sharing their understanding or asking parties to share their understandings of what has been said, and then asking questions to ensure it is accurate. When parties respond with affirmation, interest, engagement, and gestures that confirm the insights are correct, then the work of verification is done.

In mediation, both direct and inverse insights can be dramatic and exciting. But mediators and parties can also misinterpret what is going on and what is being said. Mediators remain alert to the difference between insights that have been verified and those that have not. On their own, insights do not yield full knowledge; they are only part of the full process of learning. To become knowledge, insights must be verified. Let us suppose we are walking home and observe smoke rising from a building a few streets away. We get the insight that it is our house that is burning. But this direct insight does not end the process. In fact, it likely moves us into high gear, into the operation of verifying the exact location of the fire. Verification does not provide new insights. Rather, its aim is to determine which of our ideas are correct and which are off the mark. In the case of the fire, we verify that it is down the street and not likely to cause us problems. In mediation, when we probe to confirm or reject whether, for instance, gender bias or power imbalances are fueling the dispute, we are verifying. Mediators use the strategy of verification to evoke parties' responses that either confirm or deny interpretations of what matters.

There is a curious relation between the insights of disputants and the operations of verification performed by mediators. Insight mediators often get ideas about what they think is driving a conflict or blocking the process, but until the ideas are confirmed, they cannot be sure. Their insights are not yet verified, and so they regard them as hypotheses. Then they intentionally ask questions and observe parties' responses to help confirm or reject their hypotheses. The mediator's verification is not some abstract evidence or scientific experiment; it involves close observation of the actions and reactions of the disputants themselves. When disputants make breakthroughs that clearly shift the dialogue, opening up parties' conversation in the conflict, a mediator's insights are confirmed. It is the direct and inverse insights of the disputants that provide the grounds for verifying the mediator's hypotheses. When new insights occur to parties themselves, mediators follow up on these insights to verify their meaning and significance for the conflict. The importance of verification is that mediators can rest assured they are responding to what matters to the parties themselves.

Insight mediators do the work of verification in various ways: they ask direct questions about whether what they heard or observed is correct; they look for nonverbal clues that indicate whether or not parties agree with their interpretations; they look for signs of enthusiasm or resistance when they formulate what they think matters to parties. They ask questions about the information that has led to insights. Does this information evoke a similar interest in the parties? Does it lead them to similar conclusions? If so, mediators know they are on the right track. If not, they turn their attention elsewhere. Insight mediators sometimes verify their insights simply by reading and gauging the responses of parties themselves. They also ask parties what they have come to understand or whether they have had any insights from the conversations. The most important evidence for verification occurs when parties themselves make breakthroughs that shift conflicts past blockages, opening avenues for resolution. If mediators help parties discover what really matters to them, their reactions often tell the tale.

One final point. Insight Theory helps mediators understand the difference between their efforts to understand and their role as facilitators of the parties' own understanding. In verifying her own insights, the mediator's principal concern is with parties' responses to the conflict and to each other. Of importance is what matters to the parties themselves. Mediators remain attentive to this, and Insight Theory helps them focus on both their own operations of learning and those of the parties in the conflict, so that their efforts can be directed to the parties' learning through the mediation process.

Concluding Remarks

Insight mediators are intentional about helping parties through the learning process in conflicts, and their intentionality is always focused on responding to the meanings and actions of the parties in the process. Theirs is a *responsive intentionality* rather than a directive intentionality. Insight Mediation understands conflict resolution as learning: learning about the deeper cares and concerns of others; learning about values and how they are at work in conflict; and learning about strategies for pursuing values without threatening the values of others. This learning is transformative, and it opens pathways for cooperation and resolution. Insight mediator strategies focus on facilitating this learning. Mediators seek insights and their interventions can be directive, but they do not lead parties. Their goal is to help facilitate parties' own curiosity and questioning about the things that matter to themselves and others. Insight Theory's analysis of questions, direct insights, inverse insights, verification, feelings, and values helps mediators as they negotiate their way through the learning that leads to cooperation and consensus.

5 Insight, Conflict, and Justice: Two Case Studies

Our interest throughout this book has been in exploring how Lonergan's Insight Theory advances our understanding of the learning that occurs in conflict and conflict resolution. In recent years we have observed the rise of mediation, restorative approaches to criminal justice, and participatory theories of democracy. These initiatives challenge traditional ideas about conflict and lend support to our quest for understanding in the study of conflict. Each presents an alternative to approaches that place the burden of resolving conflicts on the shoulders of authority figures. They signal a greater role for citizen involvement in dealing with the conflicts arising through the course of democratic life. We are interested in what this increased involvement requires of citizens. Our interest is in learning more about what goes on in conflict so we might equip ourselves for doing this work of conflict resolution more effectively and responsibly. Our focus has been on the learning that participants and mediators experience within conflicts when they are handled well.

Our overview of the study of conflict in chapter 2 revealed the recurring theme of learning – both the learning involved in developing skills for conflict resolution, and the learning experienced by parties within the course of conflicts. This learning can be transformative and can move parties beyond blockages, opening paths for cooperation and resolution. In chapter 3, we introduced Lonergan's Insight Theory as an innovative approach to learning. The focus was on the experience of insight and how understanding the operations of direct insight, inverse insight, and verification enhance our understanding of learning. Of particular interest was the learning involved in understanding the values carried in feelings. In chapter 4, we explored how Insight Theory helps understand the mediation model practised at Carleton University, Ottawa. Mediators in the Carleton program use strategies specifically designed to facilitate parties' learning through the process of mediation. Carleton's Insight Mediation model offers an example of Insight Theory at work: explaining the role of learning in conflict resolution, and the role of Insight Theory in understanding this learning.

Our focus in this chapter is on the resources Insight Theory can bring to the analysis of restorative justice initiatives, specifically the use of mediation and sentencing circles within the criminal justice system. Advocates of restorative justice have argued that, frequently traditional measures do not provide justice for victims of crime, nor do they help keep offenders from returning again and again to crime.[1] In an effort to explore new ways of meeting these goals, justice professionals have introduced alternative dispute resolution (ADR) practices into the system to help facilitate more direct forms of involvement of victims and community members in habilitating or rehabilitating offenders. We examine two case studies drawn from these experiences, and explore how Insight Theory helps understand what goes on when these practices meet with some success. Once again, our interest is in how Insight Theory helps understand the learning experienced when parties move past blockages and open paths for cooperative relations with others in situations involving conflict.

Our two case studies have been drawn from real-life experiences. The names of the people are changed, as are the places in which they live. The events involved in each case have been summarized, but we have sought to capture and retain the emotional and interpersonal dynamics that are evident clearly in the documentation. Both cases were recommended to us by Lorraine Berzins, the Community Chair of Justice of the Church Council on Justice and Corrections. They represent typical ways of integrating alternative measures into the justice system. The first is a victim-offender post-sentencing mediation. The second is a sentencing circle used in the context of a First Nations community. In both cases, the interventions met with some success, and our interest is in understanding what is involved in this success.

Our observations and analyses in these cases are exploratory. We believe they help illustrate the relevance of Insight Theory for understanding what is involved when alternative justice measures implicate citizens more directly in justice processes. Criminal justice brings citizens into complex forms of conflict. Traditionally, we have relied on formal procedures of lawyers and courts to deal with these conflicts on our behalf. Yet courtroom processes frequently leave many justice needs unmet, particularly those of victims, their families, and community members affected by crime.[2] Restorative justice advocates argue that these needs can be met better if victims, families, and communities become more involved in alternative justice processes. We want to know what this involvement requires of citizens. We believe that participatory approaches to criminal justice demand a great deal from citizens. In particular, we believe they require citizens' involvement in complex forms of learning that transform relationships from conflict to cooperation. If such measures are to prove sustainable, we believe this learning needs to be understood better. We offer the following case analyses in support of the relevance of Insight Theory for understanding this learning in criminal justice conflicts.

The Story of Elizabeth and Charles: A Victim-Offender Post-Sentence Mediation[3]

This case involves a woman called Elizabeth who was working in a convenience store when it was robbed by a man with a knife. She was traumatized by the experience, but according to the courts, she did not technically qualify to be considered a victim. The store's owners, who were not present during the robbery, were the only official victims. The masked robbers screamed at Elizabeth, and threatened her with death while they held a knife to her throat. She was so terrified she wet herself, and for many months after the robbers were captured, life did not return to normal for her. Stories spread about the incident, and people teased Elizabeth without mercy. Elizabeth's fear and shame began to evoke haunting memories of other traumatic events in her past, and she became ill. Instead of supporting her in her suffering, friends and family became impatient and critical. They insisted she should get on with her life. Elizabeth could not understand what was happening to her. She was ill, she had nightmares, she could not resume her life, and she became terrified whenever she closed her eyes. Her marriage broke down, and her relationship with her children deteriorated.

During all of this, the 21-year-old offender, called Charles, was serving a five-year prison sentence. He too had his own story to tell. Raised in a family environment of violence, drugs, and abuse, his only father figures were ex-offenders and addicts. He and his sisters grew up with poverty and abuse. Charles began committing minor offences as a juvenile, but this time he had crossed the line. This was his first major offence, and his sentence was being served in a federal institution. The robbery had been committed while Charles was stoned on alcohol and drugs, and to him, the event was simply the result of a very bad acid trip. He was not aware of the impact of his actions on Elizabeth, and he only learned about her trauma when he was told she insisted on submitting a victim impact statement.

Elizabeth struggled to find a way to become involved in the justice process, but apart from her victim impact statement, she continued to be excluded. She became angry and frustrated. Her memories of Charles's threats continued to haunt her, and she lived in terror that he would return to harm her. By now she had become isolated from family and friends, she lived in constant fear, and was emotionally and physically sick. She attended counselling sessions for two years, with no significant results. Finally, she realized that in order to move forward with her life, she had to bring some closure to her experiences, and to do this, she needed to find some answers to questions. So she decided to attend Charles's parole hearing.

All alone and sick with pneumonia, she boarded a bus and travelled for four hours to the institution. She was admitted to the hearing and watched with interest. At one point, Charles turned and attempted to speak to her, but an official immediately intervened and he was prevented. The rule is that at such hearings, victims and offenders are not allowed to communicate with each other. She returned home with more questions and no answers. She contacted the Parole Board, and requested a face-to-face meeting with Charles. They referred the case to a victim-offender mediation program.

When asked why she wanted this meeting with Charles, she told the mediator that she could not continue living like this. She had to get answers to her questions. She had to find out whether he was coming back to get her. She had to tell him how she felt. She had to look him in the face and tell him how he had changed her life. When the mediator told Charles of Elizabeth's fear of him, he was astonished. He said he would never have hurt her. He could not understand that store clerks never received training for this sort of thing. Weren't they instructed to simply hand over the money? Doesn't she know that every robber says: don't call the cops or I'll come back to get you? Charles was bewildered and said he was sorry for causing Elizabeth such pain.

Charles did not hesitate to agree to the meeting with Elizabeth. He was eager to do what he could to make up for what he had done. To him, the robbery had been little more than a bad night of drugs and booze, and he felt that his sentence was a heavy price to pay. He had spent two years in prison, and until this point, he had thought he was the only one suffering from the consequences of the robbery. Prison was a brutal experience. With all the stabbings going on around him, he lived in constant fear and kept a knife under his pillow at nights. But now he was learning that he was not the only person living in fear.

The mediation took place in the prison. Both Elizabeth and Charles lost sleep the night before, and both were highly charged with emotion. They met across a table and looked each other in the face. This would be their first real conversation since the robbery. Under the control of the mediator, the process began to establish its own rhythm, and they began telling their stories. Elizabeth recounted her thoughts, feelings, and experiences of the past two years while Charles listened carefully. In his turn, Charles told his own story, and answered most of Elizabeth's questions. At one point, they even began to chuckle together about a detail, and this released a lot of the tension. The talk started to become real, and they began speaking from the heart. A violent experience had brought them together into a relationship, and although their perspectives were different, they had shared something deep and profound. Much had been left unresolved since the robbery, and the mediation provided them the opportunity to begin resolving some of these things together.

What mattered to Elizabeth was that she began getting answers to questions. She learned that the real Charles was not the Charles of her nightmares and fears. She learned that he had no intention of returning to hurt her. She learned that his sorrow was genuine. She learned something of his own suffering. They came to a decision together about how they would speak to each other when they met on the street, back in their own home town, after his release. They shook hands after the mediation, and even wished each other well. Elizabeth told Charles she forgave him, and she told the mediator that the process was finished for her.

Elizabeth's nightmares and fears ended. Charles's case manager reported that he was getting along well, and was maturing after the mediation experience. Staff members felt that he would respond better to treatment, and was developing a better attitude towards life. As a final gesture of closure, Elizabeth asked that a letter be sent to the Parole Board requesting that she no longer be used as a reason for keeping Charles in jail. She said they could keep him in prison if they wanted, that was their business, but she did not want it done because of her. As far as she was concerned, it was over, she was healed.

Analysis: Applying Insight Theory to the Story of Elizabeth and Charles

There are many things going on in this case. What is clear is that the court system did not bring justice for Elizabeth. This left some of the most important elements of justice unrealized. The police did their work of apprehending the offender, and the courts did their work of finding him guilty. But the criminal justice system failed Elizabeth. Whatever else the system achieved, one major component was missing, and this component is central to our idea of what justice is all about. No one can read this case without drawing this conclusion. Elizabeth launched her own quest for justice, and she eventually attained her goals in the context of an alternative justice process, a victim-offender mediation.

The crime had a traumatic effect on Elizabeth, and it had tragic consequences that stayed with her for years after. These effects and consequences were rooted in the relationship with Charles that was created by the crime. In a technical sense, the criminal justice system did not allow Elizabeth to be considered a victim, and apart from her victim impact statement, her experiences could not be allowed to enter the orbit of the system. But she was clearly a victim, and the case highlights how the conflict created a victim-offender relationship whose transformation was central to the process of achieving justice for Elizabeth. Our analysis draws on Insight Theory to understand this transformation and the role of learning in the process. Given that the case is mostly about Elizabeth, we devote most of the analysis to her experiences. Towards the end, we offer some suggestions on how the analysis might be extended to understand the healing of Charles, the offender.

The Quest as Question

When Elizabeth climbed aboard the bus to attend Charles's parole hearing, she was embarking on a quest. To be sure, it was a quest that had begun much earlier with her efforts to present her victim impact statement and to understand her ill health, her insomnia, and her nightmares. We can assume it was a quest that extended through her counselling sessions and through her efforts to understand the deterioration of her marriage and her relations with her children. It was a quest that, in some way, she felt was thwarted when she was refused an exchange of words with Charles at the hearing. It drove her to arrange a meeting with Charles, and only came to an end when the two met and spoke face-to-face in the mediation.

The curious feature of Elizabeth's quest, however, was that until the mediation, she did not know what she was looking for. Her quest was a question. Her search was for the insights that would answer her questions. For the longest time, she had no clear understanding of what was causing her ill health and her nightmares, and she did not know what meeting Charles would achieve. Apart from the crime, she had never met Charles, and she had no idea what would happen in a conversation with him. At a certain point along the way, she did discover that she was deathly afraid of Charles returning to harm her. She also discovered that she had an urgent need to tell him how she felt and how he had harmed her life. Yet, she did not know whether her fears were grounded, what speaking to him would achieve, or whether answering any of these questions would help her heal. Elizabeth's quest, like many quests in life, was not for a known goal. It was a quest to discover, verify, and actualize an unknown. In the language of Insight Theory, her quest was a question, and her search was for insights: the direct insights of understanding herself and Charles; the inverse insights that would de-link her from the traumatizing narratives and feelings from her past; and the verification that would confirm the case closed and her healing complete.

Feelings and Values

An interesting feature of Elizabeth's quest was the difference between the surface appearance of the problem and the deeper level feelings that were moving beneath the surface of her life. On the face of it, an observer might assess her situation and conclude that little harm was done and that she ought to 'get on with her life.' She was not injured, and the offender was arrested, convicted, and sent to prison. In a formal sense, the matter was dealt with and justice was done. We can assume that many of her difficulties with friends and family arose from wrestling with such expectations. We can also assume that her own inability to 'come around' to this perspective played a role in eroding her own sense of self.

However, her feelings were not dancing to the tune of appearances; they were following their own deeper logic of values, many of which arose out of her own hidden inventory of traumatic narratives from past life experience. In the language of Insight Theory, her feelings carried hidden value narratives that evoked expectations of future harm. The fear prompted by these expectations of harm was debilitating, but as is often the case, she did not know what these value narratives were, where they came from, or how they were driving her life. She only knew that something had a grip on her and the misery this caused evoked a questioning that, in some way, had to be followed if she was to find peace.

When the mediation finally occurred, something dramatic happened to Elizabeth that brought her quest to an end and changed her life. Elizabeth learned something. She learned about Charles, about his humanity, about his real motives and his intentions for her. She learned that he had no intentions of harming her, and she had no cause to fear him. She learned he had his own legacy of suffering and injustice and his own story of the events of the crime. She learned he was genuinely sorry. And she learned about her own capacity for forgiveness. None of this learning can be understood adequately as a transfer of information. Rather, it has all the marks of the transformative learning we have understood through Insight Theory.

Direct Insights

Two distinctive features of Insight Theory need to be noted here. The first concerns the relation between Elizabeth's learning and her feelings. Her insights during the mediation were not simply answers to questions of fact. Rather, they were direct insights into values that had the effect of transforming her feelings. Her insights had the effect of unlocking or unbundling complex webs of feelings that had attached themselves to images of Charles and memories of the crime: images of Charles; troubling memories from past life experiences; and expectations about her future insecurity.

As she came to discover Charles's humanity in the mediation, these insights had the effect of replacing earlier terror-laden narratives with more realistic images of Charles the person. She came to appreciate Charles's own narrative, and this led to a new set of expectations about what might happen were they to meet again. The effect was to reconfigure her value narrative, and this shifted her patterns of feeling. Her expectations of meeting Charles on the street began to lose the terror associated with earlier images, and they began to be charged by her new-found appreciation of Charles's real humanity.

This reconfiguring of Elizabeth's inner world of feelings was achieved through insight. We can observe in this case the role of the direct insights that grasp and forge the links between images, feelings, and the data of the case. Elizabeth began to understand Charles's humanity, his own story of suffering, and his genuine sorrow. This understanding began evoking its own field of more positively charged images and feelings.

Inverse Insights

The second distinctive feature of Insight Theory involves the inverse insights that de-link Elizabeth's expectations about Charles from her terrifying memories of the crime, and her troubling memories from past life experiences. In some important way, her feelings and images of Charles get disconnected from the terror and dread from the crime. What gets de-linked is the threat. Her illness was sustained by her expectations of Charles as a threat. The compelling revelation was that the real Charles would not threaten her: his life had its own narrative path, and this narrative was not focused on harming her. Her image of Charles gets dissociated or de-linked from the fear of harm, and the result was an ability to be interested, to be curious about Charles's own story.

The de-linking transformed her relationship with Charles. As she came to discover the human Charles in the mediation, Elizabeth's way of relating to Charles, first forged in the midst of terror and violence, begins to be transformed. As he talks, she begins to listen to the story from his point of view. We can assume she begins to imagine what it might be like to 'walk in his shoes.' At the same time, she watches him listening intently to her. She watches a man, previously imaginable only as a monstrous threat, beginning to understand her, beginning to be affected emotionally by this new-found knowledge of her trauma. Something of the newly forging relationship is integral to her learning, not simply as a by-product of the learning but as constituted by the learning itself. Central to this learning is the 'un-learning' that is the inverse insight: an un-learning that de-links the previously expected necessity connecting Charles with her fear of harm.

Verification

We can also observe in this case the acts of verification operative as Charles answers the questions that confirm and verify Elizabeth's new-found understandings, feelings, and values. We can observe how this verification lays the groundwork for the decisions that forge new personal relations between Charles and Elizabeth and establish agreements for their future meeting on the streets of their home town. In all of these acts, the operations never function purely abstractly or intellectually. Rather, they function in Elizabeth as concrete reorientations of her feelings and reconfigurations of her images and patterns of valuing Charles. The result is an agreement to relate in a new way in the future, an ability to wish Charles well, and a willingness to see him released from the remainder of his sentence. None of this would be possible if Elizabeth remained doubtful about Charles's intentions.

At every step along the way through the mediation, Elizabeth's transformative learning was bound up with a transformation in her personal relationship with Charles, and her questions for Charles formed part of the process of verifying that these new patterns of relating were indeed reliable. She could count on being free from fear. What results is not a friendship, but it is a relationship that is free from fear, and more soundly rooted in a reciprocal recognition of the humanity of the other. It is this humanity that Elizabeth was able to verify to her satisfaction.

Charles the Offender

Our analysis concludes with one final note about Charles, the offender. The case does not say much about Charles but it does offer some clues about his learning. To his surprise, he discovered something of the depth of Elizabeth's suffering from the crime. He discovered something about her world. He discovered he was not the only person living in daily fear since the crime. We can assume some measure of learning in the transformed relationship that emerged in the mediation. And, if we are to believe the reports from his case manager, this learning was sufficiently maturing as to play a role in his journey towards integration into society. All of these learning moments bear the characteristics of insight, particularly the self-insight that reshapes the inner world of feelings and reorients the values carried in feelings. We can assume from the account that the personal relations that were transformed during the mediation played a role in this learning. And it would be interesting to speculate on the role her forgiveness played in shaping the longer-term directions of his life.

For our purposes, what is clear is that the mediation did indeed have an effect on Charles, and this effect was to facilitate a learning process that played a role in helping achieve one of the primary goals of the criminal justice system, the habilitation or rehabilitation of offenders. We suggest that this case illustrates the importance of the learning that transforms persons and relationships in conflict situations, and illustrates how Insight Theory can help understand what is involved in this process of learning.

What this analysis illustrates, we suggest, is the human dynamics involved in the achievement of justice in this case and the transformative power of learning in this situation of crime and conflict. The victim-offender mediation required considerable involvement by Elizabeth in order for justice to be achieved. We believe Insight Theory helps understand the dynamics of learning that played an essential role in achieving these goals. The occasions for this learning required a lot from Elizabeth. She had to do the work to get insights into herself and the offender. She had to allow her inner world of feelings and values to be transformed. To be sure, Elizabeth's pursuit of the mediation was her own initiative. No one could force her there. Yet, this too is a central feature of learning; it can only be prompted by genuine questioning. We believe there are important lessons to be learned about institutions from this line of analysis. Our interest is in pointing to key elements in the learning process and the role of Insight Theory in helping understand these elements.

The Story of Allan: A Sentencing Circle[4]

Allan, age 26, a member of the First Nation Community of Thomas River, was found guilty of carrying a weapon (a baseball bat) for the purpose of assaulting a police officer, and of theft (clothes from a home). He pled guilty to breach of probation. He had a criminal record of forty-three convictions, and had been sentenced previously to a total of eight years in jail. Common practice for the court officials who had flown in to deal with the case would have been to focus briefly on how much jail time would now be appropriate in excess of his last sentence of fifteen months. When they reviewed previous reports and assessments, however, they decided they did not want to proceed yet one more time with a criminal justice practice that had already proven a miserable failure for the community of Thomas River and for Allan himself.

Allan's background involved a history of abuse and neglect. From age ten to sixteen he lived in a series of foster homes, group homes, and juvenile centres where he experienced physical and sexual abuse. His education did not advance beyond elementary school, and consequently he never found employment. His assessments consistently described him as a person in need of extensive counselling, but to date none had been provided. With each encounter with the law, Allan grew increasingly dysfunctional and implicated in increasingly violent crime. His life had become a vicious cycle of crime, alcohol abuse, anger, mistrust, and deteriorating self-esteem. Originally from the community of Thomas River, Allan returned to his community each time he was released from jail, but with each return, the community found him less disciplined, less able to control anger or alcohol, and more of a danger to himself and his community.

If the criminal justice system had failed, what could the community do? The judge decided to adjourn for three weeks to prepare for an alternative process. He called an open meeting to discuss how the community might participate constructively in the justice system. The probation officer was asked to inquire if the First Nation and Allan's family wished to become involved. The local police officer was asked to look into the possibility of wider community involvement, and prosecuting and defence counsel were asked to consider what else might be done to break the vicious cycle that had captured Allan. The court decided to make changes to the process before, during, and after sentencing to allow wider community involvement in addressing the issues and their impacts.

Before the sentencing hearing, the probation officer met with the chief and other First Nations members as well as the accused and his family, to encourage their help in breaking this cycle. The prosecuting attorney visited community members to become familiar with their concerns. Considerable work was invested by counsel, probation officers, and community members in exploring and developing proposals for sentencing before the sentencing hearing.

For the hearing, the physical arrangement of the courtroom was changed to a circle seating thirty people. The formal process was transformed into an intense interpersonal discussion of what might best protect the community and help Allan find his way out of the grip of alcohol and crime. Left behind were the formalities of the courtroom, and in their place, participants experienced a setting where community members could speak directly to Allan about the personal impacts of his actions. For the first time, Allan heard his family and community tell him how they felt victimized by his crimes.

Allan's family openly discussed their concerns. Allan's mother, his brother, the chief of the First Nation, the police, the probation officer, and other community members who had known him all his life were able to share their views, and they expressed constructive concern about Allan. They repeatedly spoke of the need to reintegrate Allan with his family and his First Nation. This was the first time Allan had heard anyone from his community speak this way. They were offering welcome and support, not criticism and rejection. For the first time, the chief and other First Nation members offered their time and resources to help reintegrate Allan. This aggressively positive expression from all participants sent a message of belonging to Allan. It was a message saying they wanted him to be part of their lives. This had a dramatic impact on Allan. Much of his hostility and anger began to drain away.

For years, Allan had believed that the community wanted him to leave, that they wanted him to take his troubles elsewhere. In the sentencing circle, Allan heard a dramatically different message. He could no longer believe that the police and the community were solely interested in removing him from their midst. The comments from his community drew Allan into the discussion. His eloquence, passion, and pain rivetted everyone's attention. He did not convince everyone, nor was he able to achieve what he had hoped in his sentence. But the ability to communicate frankly, passionately, and directly within the circle contributed to constructing a novel sentence that would have important positive consequences for Allan.

There were three objectives for Allan's sentence: protecting the community, rehabilitating the offender, and minimizing adverse impacts on victims. The circle members forged a collective desire for something different, something unlike the sentences imposed in past years, something everyone could support, something they believed would work. The information shared in the circle, particularly about the underlying causes of criminal behaviour, convinced everyone that in addition to formal sentencing remedies, community resources also needed to be mobilized. Having acquired first-hand knowledge of community concerns, and armed with detailed life information about the offender, the prosecuting attorney was able to assess how the interests of the state and community could best be addressed in sentencing. Defence counsel was able to use the circle constructively to develop a sentencing plan to advance the immediate and long term interests of his client. The result was that community support was offered to provide a viable alternative to jail.

The probation officer described vividly why, despite common perceptions that Allan had been given many chances for rehabilitation in the past, Allan persisted in believing that he had never been given a chance. Most of Allan's chances were incorporated in a probation order that came into play upon the termination of a lengthy jail sentence. Allan's intentions to change his life at the time of sentencing were obliterated by jail. His self-image, courage, and will to change were drained by his experience in jail. Upon his release, he easily fell back into his pattern of good times, bad company, and substance abuse, and with this came the return of feelings of despondency, defeat, and anger. Would probation work without jail? No, that too had a record of failure. If not jail, if not probation, then what?

The judge concluded that for any prospect of rehabilitation, something other than punishment, something other than jail, needed to be used. The justice system's repertoire of resources for rehabilitation had proven inadequate. Like many repeat offenders, the circumstances perpetuating Allan's life of crime arose not just from substance abuse, but from his overall life situation. Any successful rehabilitative investment would need to embrace much more than simply substance abuse. The offender's entire life circumstances had to be addressed. Alone, Allan had no chance. His impoverished, socially deprived lifestyle precluded him from effectively utilizing justice or community resources. The question now became: how can the community's involvement change this pattern?

Allan's First Nation and his family responded to the challenge. Their involvement provided the main opening for focusing the sentence on rehabilitation. In the circle, they recognized the role they could provide in healing and helping a member of their community. From this recognition grew a sentence focused on rehabilitation and reliant mainly upon family and community resources. Their creative search produced a sentence markedly different from Allan's past experience and from customary sentences for such crimes.

So what happened? The three months spent in remand awaiting trial was deemed sufficient punishment. A suspended sentence coupled with a two-year probation order provided the legal framework for a three-part sentencing plan. First, the offender was required to live with his family on their trapline sixty miles out of town. His family would ensure that a family member stayed with him. Second, he was to attend a two-month residential program for Native alcoholics. Third, he was to be brought back to his family, who would provide an alcohol-free home, and to the First Nation, who would provide a support program to help him upgrade life and employment skills. The First Nation would also provide continued substance abuse counselling. He would also be counselled by his probation officer, and would receive assistance in finding a job. At each stage, a court review would be held in the circle to fine-tune the plan and offer further support. For the first time in his life, Allan would be serving a sentence he had helped construct. The circle played a key role in allowing Allan and his community to speak frankly, openly, and directly to each other about the things that mattered to them. The result was a novel path of justice for Allan, and an opportunity for community involvement and support in living this out.

Analysis: Applying Insight Theory to the Story of Allan

This case allows us to focus on the role of learning in achieving justice in a community context. We know that the innovative sentence resulted in some important transformations in the life of the offender, Allan. We can only speculate on what this learning involved and how it unfolded in the years following. What the case does provide is considerable detail on a significant moment in the justice process, the sentencing circle itself. Our analysis will focus on the circle, how it involved transformative learning, the role of the judge in this learning, how the community played a key role in this learning, and how Insight Theory helps us understand this learning and its contribution to justice.

The Quest and the Questioning

When Allan was found guilty, the judge knew that the normal course of events would be to sentence Allan to more jail time, and this, he knew, would only accelerate the cycle of violence. He could not allow this to happen, but he did not know what else to do. Faced with this unknown, what he did was to launch a quest – a questioning process that sought to know something he did not already know; a learning process. He adjourned the court for three weeks to allow the probation officer, the local police, the prosecutor, and the defence attorney to involve members of the wider community in exploring alternative ways of achieving the goals of justice. He did not know what these might be, but he decided it was time to find out. They proposed a sentencing circle in which Allan, his family, members of his First Nation, and members of his community would join the court in a process of discussing, deliberating, and deciding on the sentence. Again, no one knew what would happen in the circle. We can observe two steps in this questioning process: the first, in which the judge launched his quest to understand and decide on how best to proceed; and the second, the circle itself, in which Allan, the court, and the community sought to understand and decide on the sentence. This two-step questioning process, we suggest, made the difference in achieving a more suitable path of justice for Allan and the community.

We can observe how the learning process involved the active engagement of the learner and the learning community in the pursuit of an unknown. The essence of this quest is questioning. The process of venturing into new horizons of justice was precipitated by the judge's decision to involve himself in a new way in the lives of Allan and the community. He refused to allow the justice system to continue in its standard routines, and instead, he launched an active pursuit for something new, something that at the outset was unknown. We can observe here one of the essential elements of Lonergan's Insight Theory. Learning is neither the passive reception of information, nor is it simply the constructive work of reason, imagination, or social forces. It is a discovery process that requires the engagement of learners in the activity of questioning, their immersion in the relevant experiential fields, and their openness to receiving new possibilities in the form of insight. This engagement requires a decision to search for new solutions – a decision that admits the old solutions to be inadequate, and a decision that takes responsibility both for the problem and for the inquiry process itself. This is precisely what the judge did.

At a certain point, Allan became actively engaged in this quest. Like most offenders, he had never before participated actively in his own sentencing. Before the circle, his behaviour suggested little more than anger and contempt towards the justice process. But something happened in the circle that changed all this. For the first time, Allan was provided a context for speaking in his own voice to a community willing and able to understand him. He was provided some credible assurance that what he said could affect his future in a significant way. His community members gave him every indication that they were interested in what he had to say. This was a new experience. More than this, he heard something new from them. Contrary to prior expectations, Allan heard his community tell him firmly and strongly that they wanted him back as a fully functioning member and that the court wanted nothing more than to have this happen.

The effect on Allan was to shift the form of his engagement and he became an active participant in the quest for solutions. Once a hostile observer of the machineries of justice, Allan became an active participant, more hopeful about his role in shaping his own sentence, more assured of his membership in the community, and now for the first time, more confident that he might play a real role in reshaping his life. There can be no doubt that everyone in the court observed this transformation in Allan. The judge noted this change in Allan and linked it to the innovative approach to the sentencing process. By engaging in the circle with curiosity, interest, and passion, Allan played a role in shaping his own sentence, and this laid the groundwork for his active engagement in the learning that would begin to change his life. We suggest that this engagement bears all the marks of the questioning that is central to the transformative learning of Insight Theory.

Direct Insights

Through both stages of the learning process – the initial community consultations that led to the circle, and the discussions and deliberations within the circle itself – we can observe the innovative role of insight. The judge knew that the court faced a situation where business as usual could only end in deteriorating conditions for the offender and increased danger to the community. The justice system was not working. It had no inventory of reasonable strategies and no source of alternative ideas. What it needed was new insights, and the search for these insights was the process the judge launched.

What he and the community achieved was more than simply a new outcome; it was an insight into how the learning process itself could function to achieve innovative outcomes within the justice system. The decision to adjourn the court and launch the community consultation resulted in the insight to establish the circle. This insight to hold the circle established a second learning context. In this newly devised context, Allan and the entire community would play significant roles in achieving the insights that would lead to his novel sentencing strategy. What this case illustrates is not simply the significance of insight, but how insight can reflect upon and transform the very process of gaining insights. Learning about the process of learning transformed the justice process for all.

We can observe how the community played a key role in gathering the experiential data both for the process design and for the learning that occurred within the circle itself. We can observe the insights that the court needed in order to understand the circle, its roots in Aboriginal traditions, its relevance to the current context, and the demands it would make on the court, the offender, and the community. We can observe the insights achieved within the circle: these insights would transform the court's inventory of sentencing alternatives, and the offender's sense of engagement in the process. We can observe the verification process, with its evaluative questions and its weighing of evidence, a process that would lead to the court's judgment on the adequacy of the sentence. Finally, we can observe the role of all of these insights in shaping the court's final decision to risk adopting the innovative strategy in the interests of justice for Allan and his community.

An important feature of insight in this case is the role of personal relationships in establishing the experiential base for achieving insight, and the role of insight in transforming relationships within the justice process. From the beginning of the process, the judge recognized that there was a link between the system's failure and its standard routines of formal, faceless relationships. He speaks of how the formal roles of justice professionals insulate them from experiencing the full humanity of the drama unfolding before them. He speaks of the way the system sets offenders in formal, adversarial relations with the state, thereby insulating them from the human reality of the pain and suffering they have caused. But he also speaks of the dramatic role played by the parole officer who took the initiative to help shift the system out of its faceless, mechanical routines to engage the personal relations that would help change the process and the life of Allan and the community. The insight to place the system on a new learning path brought the justice professionals into new forms of personal engagement with the offender and the community, and this provided the experiential base for the insights that would change the way Allan, the court, and the community would begin to relate to each other within the circle and in the months and years following.

Inverse Insights

One of the important transformative moments in the circle occurred when the community members expressed their strong gesture of support for Allan's return and reintegration into the community of Thomas River. This involved an inverse insight de-linking of Allan's expectations from the feelings and value narratives of harm and humiliation arising from past experiences with the justice system. To this point, Allan's experience of the justice system was of a formal, faceless process. Offenders are tried, examined, and often defended by strangers who assume professionally staged roles in a highly ritualized setting. Their offences are declared to be crimes against the state rather than against real people. Their actions, motives, and life experiences are described and debated by strangers in a language that bears no relation to their own self-understanding. The result of the court's procedures is for these strangers to impose blame, shame, and punishment on them for experiences that, in the eyes of the offender, they have failed totally to understand.

The effect of all this is to create for offenders an unreal value narrative about the meaning of what they have done. Without a real experiential encounter with their victims, they are permitted to live with illusions about the justice of their actions. And within the ritual formalities of the court system, this narrative comes to portray the court as the oppressor. The result is a sustained expectation that justice means harm and humiliation. For Allan, however, all this started to change when members of his community began to speak. For the first time, he heard people he knew speak in a language he understood of the real pain and suffering he had caused in his community. For the first time, he heard them tell him in strong and clear words that he belonged, that they wanted him healed, that they wanted him back with them to help them build the community. Integral to Allan's learning was the inverse insight, de-linking him from the expectations of harm and humiliation associated with his prior experiences of the justice system. For the first time, he was able to de-link from the feelings of apathy, contempt, and disengagement arising from his past experiences, and the result was an openness to encountering his community in new ways.

Feelings and Values

Allan's transformation involves two moments, perhaps not discrete or separate in time, but different enough in their function to warrant understanding them as different and complementary components in the transformative process of learning. The first is the inverse insight, de-linking him from the feelings of apathy and contempt and the expectations of harm and humiliation associated with past experiences of the justice system. The second is the new insight with its feelings of community belonging and the newly emerging value narrative that would reorient his thinking about the justice of his own sentence. In both of these moments, we can observe the significance of feelings and values in establishing Allan's relation to his community and the justice system.

What Allan experienced in the circle was an insight into the links between his actions and its human consequences for his victims and the community, and this linkage became charged with real human feelings. He also achieved an insight into the way they valued him, and this opened an entire vista of feelings that previously he could not have imagined. What gave way, what became de-linked, was his older understanding of the meaning of the court, his trial, his offence, and his sentence.

What is significant is not simply the change in feelings, but the links between the feelings and the values that they are about. Allan's new-found sense of belonging was a feeling about his own self-worth, this time supported strongly by people he respected. His new feeling of sorrow for the harm he had caused was a feeling about their worth in his eyes. And we can assume that his new-found openness to engaging in the proceedings of the circle was linked to a new respect for the value of the court itself and its relationship to his real community. We can observe here the subtle interplay between insight, feelings, and values that is at the heart of the transformative learning that occurs when conflict resolution processes meet with success.

Learning and Community

Finally, this case highlights the role of the community in the transformative learning that is central to justice. Learning is a highly personal matter but its conditions and consequences are fully social. What became clear to the judge was that nothing could have changed for Allan without the community's support. The only option open was another jail term, and the consequences of that were all too clear. Allan needed something to change in his life but, given the shape of his life experiences, he was in no position to effect this change on his own. What he needed was support, guidance, mentoring, and only the community could provide this.

For Allan to learn required the court to learn, and this too could only happen with the input of the community. What the circle achieved was a favourable context for the community's input into a transformative learning process, both for the court and for Allan. This process would establish the wider social context for Allan's rehabilitation. This required a shift in focus of the court itself, from punishment to rehabilitation. It required the mobilization of community resources that, typically, would not have been considered their concern. It required a large number of personal conversations to establish mutual trust between the court and the community. It required an openness of the judge and the court to an alternative that, otherwise, would be thought absurd. All these events contributed to weaving the web of relations that would mobilize the community to become an active participant in resolving conflict and achieving justice. We suggest that Insight Theory helps understand the learning involved in this community justice process

Concluding Remarks

Our goal in these two case studies has been to draw upon Insight Theory to help understand the learning involved when alternative justice processes meet with some measure of success. We believe it is important to understand this learning – how it works, how it involves citizens in achieving justice, and how it shapes our understanding of justice. Crimes involve conflict, and dealing adequately with the personal and community relations involved in this conflict is an important part of achieving justice. We suggest this requires understanding the learning involved in conflict resolution, and we offer this analysis of Insight Theory as a resource for pursuing this understanding.

Central to these two case analyses are the operations of questions, feelings and values, direct insights, inverse insights, and verification in the learning process. Learning is personal, but it is also interpersonal and communal. It is transformative, and gaining direct and inverse insights into the value narratives carried in feelings can have the effect of reshaping feelings and transforming relationships. We suggest that these two cases reveal the importance of this transformative learning in achieving justice. Of particular importance in the second case is the learning achieved by the judge, and how this learning reshaped the opportunities for new forms of citizen participation in the justice process. This participation resulted in the offender and the community making their own contributions to the transformative learning that was central to achieving justice in this case.

One final note. We believe that this analysis invites new directions in thinking about conflict resolution within justice institutions. We argue that understanding justice as conflict resolution and understanding conflict resolution as transformative learning requires reassessing the formal, non-participatory character of many of our justice processes.

Resolving conflicts involves healing personal and community relationships, and for this to happen, participants need to become involved much more directly. Justice processes need to allow and facilitate this participation. These two case studies illustrate how mediation and sentencing circles can work within and alongside the existing system to achieve this participation. To be sure, this sort of participation requires a great deal from citizens, perhaps more than many of us would wish. Still, we believe that rethinking the future of justice processes should be led by understanding, and we offer this analysis of Insight Theory in an effort to advance this understanding.

6 Concluding Reflections

In her compelling study of cities and economies, Jane Jacobs painted an extraordinary portrait of the role of insight, innovation, and problem solving in the economic and cultural life of city regions.[1] Meandering through city neighbourhoods, she observed how the 'eyes on the street' of citizens ensure the security of children in ways that could never be achieved by police working alone. What citizens learn are the potential threats to neighbourhood security that arise in the course of ordinary life and the myriad ways these threats can be averted through the mobilization of interested community members. She observed how city economies grow to maturity and resist decline through countless acts of insight and innovation in which women and men adapt to new challenges, replace imports, develop new exports, and turn existing resources to the solution of new problems. Jacobs made insight a central focus of more than four decades of her work.[2] She called city planners, economists, and governments to pay close attention to these acts of insight and innovation. And she helped us all understand how cultures develop and resist decline through the countless acts of insight of its citizens.

We believe it is time to begin thinking this way about conflict. Our explorations through the chapters of this book share Jacobs's interest in insight. Our focus is on conflict and the contributions of Insight Theory to understanding the learning that goes on when conflicts are resolved well. With Jacobs, we believe there is something important to be gained from thinking anew about our involvement in conflict and how policies and institutions can support this work of transforming conflict through insight. We learn our way through the conflicts of life. We believe it is time to think more broadly about the implications of this learning for democratic life.

There is an integral link between conflict and democracy. Democratic societies are pluralist, and pluralism means conflicts among people of diverse cultures, religions, philosophies, and values. We like to think of ours as peaceful societies where toleration and the rule of law prevail. Yet, more than any others, democratic societies place citizens in situations where we must live day-to-day with the conflicts arising from different traditions and convictions. Achieving this peace requires dealing with these conflicts. We often pride ourselves in our ability to 'live and let live.' But democratic societies have the curious tendency to draw us, time and again, into intense interaction with others in neighbourhoods, public processes, family relations, and multicultural workplaces. In many of these interactions, we cannot simply set aside our differences; we must confront them and work through them. This brings us into conflict. Many of the debates among theorists of democracy are about how to deal with these conflicts.[3]

In recent decades, we have watched the rise of mediation, restorative justice, and participatory democracy. In each of these we observe an alternative to more traditional approaches that placed the burden of resolving conflicts on the shoulders of authority figures. We believe that the rise of these alternative approaches signals a greater role for citizens in dealing with the conflicts arising through the course of our lives. Our interest through these chapters is in exploring the role of learning in working through these conflicts. If this work of citizen learning is to be supported by social and political institutions, we need to do some innovative thinking about insight and learning.

There is another reason we believe insight is important for understanding conflict. There is something in the way we commonly think about democracy that can undermine our commitment to learning in conflicts. Popular ideas about democracy seem to absolve us of the responsibility of working through conflicts. How often do we hear responses like, 'This is a free country!' when ideas or actions are challenged? This sort of comment is often used to justify disengaging from conversation when ideas and values conflict. There is a prevailing assumption that democracy means nothing more than free elections, free markets, and equal rights, and freedom and equality require admitting that value conflicts are not to be resolved.[4] Conversation in situations of conflict cannot be expected to achieve anything of value, and so we disengage. Often this is heralded as the great virtue of toleration.[5]

But this response causes considerable trouble when one person's 'free choice' disrupts the lives of others. In such cases, our first reflex is to turn to lawyers and courts. And, in some way, we believe this is what democracy is all about. If we are wealthy, we can hire experts to navigate the justice system to our advantage. But if we are not, we encounter the radical flaws in this way of thinking. There is something costly, inefficient, traumatic, unjust, hurtful, and profoundly untrue about this way of living with each other. Yet, we hang onto ideas of democracy that seem to bolster this way of traumatizing each other.

In the past two decades, philosophers and political theorists have begun to rethink basic ideas about conflict and democracy, and we believe that Insight Theory offers an important contribution to these conversations. Philosophers like Joshua Cohen and Jürgen Habermas have proposed that democracy be understood not simply as freedom and equality, but as a deliberative process in which we work out our differences in communication with our fellow citizens.[6] They argue that understanding the social structure of communication can help in formulating guidelines that can help parties as they work their way through the conflicts of democratic deliberation.[7] We suggest, however, that we not only *learn about* communication in conflicts, but that we also *learn within* communication in conflicts, and we can *learn about learning* in conflicts. Because learning is transformative, we can even learn from others from diverse traditions. Understanding this learning, we suggest, offers a new dimension to the deliberative approach to conflict and democracy.

Our interest is in the learning activity that goes on within good conversations, particularly when this learning enables parties to surmount obstacles and deal cooperatively with conflicts. When conversations work well, parties learn from each other, and this learning transforms their sense of themselves and each other. It was the transformative feature of learning that captured the attention of Jack Mezirow and his associates. Following Habermas, Mezirow studied the social dynamics of this learning. But while transformative learning has a social side, it also has a personal side. And we have followed the invitation of William Rehg to turn to the work of Lonergan to understand how insight works to transform ideas, feelings, and attitudes towards each other.

We believe that Insight Theory and Insight Mediation offer a body of theory and experience in support of this line of reflection on conflict and learning. At the centre of the Insight approach is the mediator's work of facilitating parties' insights into cares and threats. Democratic societies are places where citizens from diverse cultures and traditions are thrust together in the task of building families, neighbourhoods, workplaces, community organizations, cities, economies, and political societies. This engagement can be intense, and it makes democracies prone to conflict. Insight Mediation teaches us that our first response to conflict will be to focus on surface issues, holding fast to positions. It teaches us that we will be dynamized by feelings that carry cares and threats that remain obscure and hidden, and that value narratives from the past will give rise to feelings of threat that distort our understanding of the cares of others. Given this experience, we can expect to encounter difficulties when we wrestle with issues on this superficial level. Insight Mediation invites us to understand why this is so and to turn our attention to deeper levels of feelings and values.

Insight Mediation invites us to become curious about ourselves and our partners in conflict. It invites us to follow the lead of mediators and probe our own feelings and those of others for insights into the deeper cares and threats undergirding our positions. It invites us to wonder whether our values might be pursued in ways that need not threaten those of others. It invites us to resist the urge to demonize our adversaries and to begin imagining them anew, as ordinary persons with cares and concerns like our own. It invites us to invoke the inverse insights that de-link our expectations of threat from our own legitimate cares and those of others, and to begin wondering how we might pursue our values in ways that do not threaten those of others.

What we also learn from Insight Mediation is that this work is quite difficult. It requires devoting ourselves to the hard work of developing new habits and skills. It requires that we have the presence of mind to invite the assistance of third parties – not to do this work for us, but to help us work out solutions for ourselves when we encounter obstacles we cannot surmount on our own. It requires thinking longer-term about the cultural, educational, and media supports for cultivating these habits and skills on a wider scale.

Most important, all of this requires that we admit the significance of citizens doing this work of learning for democratic societies to function well. We believe that Insight Mediation offers an important corrective to common attitudes. Contrary to popular opinion, democracy is not simply about freedom and equality. To be sure, these values are important, but they are only the beginning. Free societies invariably become complex societies, and this places significant demands on citizens. It is citizens who must negotiate social complexity, difference, and social change. Without this, societies do not flourish.

Negotiating social complexity means negotiating conflict, and we believe that understanding the learning involved in resolving conflict requires that we begin thinking differently about our responsibilities towards each other. For democratic life to thrive requires that citizens be willing and prepared to do the hard work of learning in conflict, and Insight Theory helps us understand what is involved in this learning.

Our journey through the chapters of this book has taken us from an overview of the history of conflict research to an introduction to Lonergan's Insight Theory and its application to mediation and the use of mediation and sentencing circles within the criminal justice system. Our central idea is that conflict resolution involves learning, and Lonergan's Insight Theory enhances our understanding of this learning. To be sure, our focus is not the learning of classrooms and textbooks; it is the learning we experience in ordinary life, in our interactions with family, loved ones, neighbours, coworkers, and fellow citizens. Most important, it is the learning that transforms feelings and reshapes relationships in conflict. We believe that understanding insight helps us think more wisely and creatively about our role as participants in resolving the conflicts of democratic life.

Our attention in these chapters has been directed to the interpersonal and small group conflicts that arise through the course of everyday life. We have not addressed the challenges arising in violent conflict, oppression, war, or genocide. We believe there is much to be learned from a careful understanding of simpler conflicts that can provide resources and direction for the more difficult work. Consequently, our efforts have focused on more basic ideas. What we find, however, is that the simpler conflicts are actually more complex than we had thought. We suggest that understanding this complexity may well prove helpful in wrestling with the more difficult conflicts that galvanize our thinking about social and political life.

Insight Theory and Insight Mediation teach us something about this complexity. Learning cannot be understood simply as the transfer of information. It is a complex set of operations that unfolds on four levels: experience, understanding, verification, and decision. It involves multiple feedback loops and circles that cycle and recycle us through the four levels of operations. Learning is transformative, and it alters feelings and relationships. It involves immersion in experience, but it also requires the direct insights that answer questions about experience and transform us from confusion to comprehension. Insights are answers to questions, and to yield insights, questions must be on the right track. So learning also involves the inverse insights that de-link us from misleading expectations and shift us from one line of questioning to another.

For learning in conflict to bear fruit, it must involve insights into cares and threats, and this means the linking insights that grasp value narratives operative in feelings, as well as the de-linking insights that move us beyond the blockages caused by feelings of threat. Insights are never isolated events; they cluster together to yield reference frames or horizons, and understanding others requires gaining insights into the horizons that frame their questioning and valuing. Learning also involves verifying insights, and it involves making the decisions that commit us to action and bring about the new experiences that launch us into the next cycle of learning.

Most important, learning about learning requires understanding the curious character of insight: how we must pursue it in questioning but still await its arrival. Insights often catch us by surprise and transform our patterns of thinking and feeling. But they do so in ways that make it difficult to advert to the transformation moment itself. Understanding the transformative character of insight requires careful attention to our own operations of understanding. It requires getting past the obstacles posed by misleading images. It requires cultivating the habits and skills required for the double focus of attention involved in self-understanding: attending to the challenge before us, and attending to our operations of insight. Like all skills, the method of self-understanding is awkward and difficult at first, but it can be learned. We argue that it is worth learning, for the sake of our relations with family, friends, and neighbours, and for the sake of our democracies that depend on our ability to work through the conflicts of everyday life.

One final point. At the centre of Insight Theory and Insight Mediation is an attitude that needs to be cultivated if we are to gain insights into learning in conflict. This attitude is curiosity. Our curiosity needs to be genuine, and it needs to focus, not only on others but also on ourselves. When Insight mediators help us probe for insights into cares and threats, what we discover are value narratives that previously we had not recognized or understood. What was driving our behaviour in the conflict was something that was a mystery to us. Resolving conflicts requires acknowledging this mystery and responding with curiosity.

We suggest that curiosity needs to become a focal point of the larger conversation about conflict. This is because curiosity is the heart of learning in conflict, and there are many ways it can become blocked or damaged. It can be blocked by feelings of threat and certainty. It can become damaged by manipulation and self-interest. It can be poisoned by cynicism and scepticism. Genuine curiosity is central to learning, and it needs to become part of the conflict conversation, both as a topic, and a mode of engagement. Genuine curiosity is hopeful, but not naive. It admits complexity, but is not discouraged by challenge. Most of all, it is willing to admit we do not already have the answers.

There is much to learn about learning, and we believe Insight Theory can contribute to the study of learning in conflict. We learn our way through the conflicts of democratic life, and we believe there is much to be gained from understanding this learning. Conflict presents challenges for our personal relations, our justice institutions, and our involvement in democracy. Citizens play a significant role in resolving these conflicts. We offer these explorations in the hope that learning becomes a topic in the field of conflict studies. We believe that Insight Theory can be helpful in furthering conversations in the field, and Insight Mediation can advance democracy's work of transforming conflict through insight.

Notes

1 Conflict and Insight: Setting the Stage

1 Lonergan's principal philosophical work is *Insight: A Study of Human Understanding*. Other significant philosophical works include *Understanding and Being*, *Phenomenology and Logic*, *Philosophical and Theological Papers 1958–1964*, and *Philosophical and Theological Papers 1965–1980*. Secondary works that provide helpful introductions to Lonergan include Flanagan, *Quest for Self-Knowledge*; Melchin, *Living with Other People*; Mathews, *Lonergan's Quest*; and Meynell, *Introduction to the Philosophy of Bernard Lonergan*. For secondary works that situate Lonergan within wider conversations in philosophy, see McCarthy, *The Crisis of Philosophy*; Fitzpatrick, *Philosophical Encounters*; Crysdale, *Lonergan and Feminism*; Meynell, *Redirecting Philosophy*; and Braman, *Meaning and Authenticity*. Lonergan's work also includes significant contributions to theology, and theological works that provide rich resources for our analyses through the chapters of this book include *Method in Theology*, and *Topics in Education*. See the bibliography for other relevant Lonergan texts.
2 For on-line resources that provide access to scholarly literature applying Lonergan to diverse fields of experience, see http://www.ustpaul.ca/lonergancentre; http://www.bc.edu/bc_org/avp/cas/lonergan; http://lonergan.concordia.ca; http://www.lonergan-lri.ca/index1.shtml; http://www.shu.edu/catholic-mission/lonergan.
3 See Picard et al., *The Art and Science of Mediation*, 35–8.
4 See ibid., 42–50.
5 Of course, parties do not always agree with adjudicators' rulings. Adjudication often provides for an appeal process that can overturn rulings. When this happens, laws specify the form of compliance required until the appeal

takes its course. The point here is that, even when parties disagree with adjudicators' rulings, they are expected to comply with the law, and this compliance involves some shift in attitude within them. This shift involves some element of learning, and our interest is in the various ways that learning is involved in the resolution process.

6 For a fascinating study that draws on Lonergan to analyse the discovery process in legal decision-making, see Anderson, *Discovery in Legal Decision-Making*.

7 See Picard et al., *The Art and Science of Mediation*, chap. 10.

8 See ibid.

9 It is interesting to note that the retributive model makes important assumptions about the public character of justice and the learning involvement of citizens in achieving justice. When crimes are committed, we are satisfied that justice has been done when we learn that offenders have been apprehended and been made to pay for their offence. Our learning here is a type of ethical learning that a wrong has been made right. There is also the social learning involved in deterrence. We assume that punishment helps us learn that crime does not pay. Finally, we assume that offenders learn from punishment. We might challenge the validity of these assumptions or whether our justice system achieves these learning objectives, but what is important here is not the validity or performance of the system, but the assumptions of the model. We can observe similar sorts of learning assumptions in the other snapshots. The implication, here, is that wide-scale public learning is involved dramatically in the adjudication model of conflict, the retributive model of justice, and the Hobbes-based model of democracy. We have not developed these analyses in order to focus on the learning involved in the alternative models. Still, we are convinced the implications are enormous for future research on conflict, justice, and democracy.

10 For a discussion of diverse approaches to democracy see Melchin, 'Reaching Toward Democracy.' See also Hobbes, *Leviathan*, chaps 14–15; and Wolin, 'Fugitive Democracy,' 31–3. See the discussion of Jean-Jacques Rousseau by Jürgen Habermas in 'Three Normative Models,' and 'Popular Sovereignty as Procedure.' See also Benhabib, introduction, in *Democracy and Difference*, 5–6.

11 Wolin, 'Fugitive Democracy,' 42.

12 Hobbes, *Leviathan*, chaps 14–15; Wolin, 'Fugitive Democracy,' 31–3.

13 Habermas, 'Three Normative Models.'

14 Bohman and Rehg, introduction, in *Deliberative Democracy*, ix–xxx, in particular, x. See also Habermas, 'Popular Sovereignty as Procedure.'

15 Habermas, 'Three Normative Models,' 22.

16 We recognize that the conversation has moved on from the debate between liberals and communitarians. The concern now is multiculturalism and the diversity of traditions. Our point here is to draw out assumptions about conflict and learning operative in popular ideas about democracy. The challenges of multiculturalism and democracy are discussed more fully further on in this chapter and in chapter 6.

17 Recent conversations on 'deliberative democracy' highlight this growing attention to citizen participation in public life. See, e.g., Benhabib, *Democracy and Difference*; and Bohman and Rehg, *Deliberative Democracy*.

18 For a compelling analysis of postmodernism that draws on Lonergan, see Lawrence, 'The Fragility of Consciousness.'

19 The most notable of these are G.W.F. Hegel and Karl Marx.

20 See, e.g., Tjosvold, introduction, in *Managing Conflict*; Deutsch, 'A Theoretical Perspective on Conflict and Conflict Resolution'; and Coser, *The Functions of Social Conflict*.

21 See, e.g., Young, 'Communication and the Other,' 'Difference as a Resource for Democratic Communication,' and *Throwing Like a Girl*, in particular, chaps 6 and 7. See also Benhabib, 'Toward a Deliberative Model of Democratic Legitimacy,' and her introduction in *Democracy and Difference*, 11–14.

22 See, e.g., Cranton, *Understanding and Promoting Transformative Learning*.

23 For overviews of various schools of learning theory, see, e.g., Finger and Asún, *Adult Education at the Crossroads*; Elias and Merriam, *Philosophical Foundations of Adult Education*; and Merriam and Caffarella, *Learning in Adulthood*.

24 Cranton, *Transformative Learning*, 22–3.

25 See Cranton, *Transformative Learning*; Mezirow, 'Critical Reflection'; and Marsick, 'Action Learning and Reflection in the Workplace.'

26 Cranton, *Transformative Learning*, 29–40.

27 Ibid., 46–51.

28 See Mezirow, 'Critical Reflection,' 8–11.

29 Cranton, *Transformative Learning*, 72–7.

30 Mezirow, 'Critical Reflection,' 13–14.

31 Rehg, *Insight and Solidarity*.

32 Ibid., 84.

33 See notes no. 1 and 2, above, for relevant primary and secondary Lonergan literature as well as the bibliography. In chapter 3, we present a more detailed analysis of Lonergan's Insight Theory, and the references direct readers to primary and second literature on diverse aspects of Lonergan's philosophy.

2 Studying Conflict

1 Boulding, foreword, in *Conflict Management*.
2 See, e.g., Meadows et al., *Limits to Growth*.
3 See, Boulding, foreword, in *Conflict Management*; Wedge, introduction, in *Conflict Management*; and Sandole, introduction, in *Conflict Management*.
4 See, Boulding, foreword, in *Conflict Management*, ix.
5 Tjosvold, introduction, in *Managing Conflict*.
6 Coser, *Functions of Social Conflict*.
7 See Berger, *Invitation to Sociology*, 93–121 and 183–4.
8 See, e.g., Hegel, *Lectures on the Philosophy of World History*; and Marx, 'Economic and Philosophic Manuscripts of 1844.'
9 See Giddens, *New Rules of Sociological Method*, 54–70, 98–104.
10 See, e.g., Habermas, 'Three Normative Models,' and 'Popular Sovereignty.'
11 Burton, *World Society*, cited in Deutsch, 'Theoretical Perspective,' 38.
12 Deutsch, 'Theoretical Perspective,' 38.
13 Tjosvold, 'Interdependence Approach,' 44–5; see also, Deutsch, 'Theoretical Perspective,' 42–4.
14 Tjosvold, 'Interdependence Approach,' 43; see also, Deutsch, 'Theoretical Perspective,' 42–4.
15 Tjosvold, 'Interdependence Approach,' 45–50; see also, Bergmann and Volkema, 'Understanding and Managing Interpersonal Conflict at Work.'
16 See Kremenyuk, 'The Emerging System.'
17 Deutsch, 'Theoretical Perspective,' 46–7.
18 Siebe, 'Game Theory.'
19 Kremenyuk, 'The Emerging System,' 22.
20 Raiffa, 'Contributions of Applied Systems Analysis to International Negotiation,' 7–11, and *The Art and Science of Negotiation*, 2–4.
21 Kremenyuk, 'The Emerging System,' 30.
22 Ibid., 37.
23 Raiffa, *The Art and Science of Negotiation*, 1–6.
24 Galbraith, back cover of *Getting to Yes*, by Fisher and Ury.
25 Fisher and Ury, *Getting to Yes*, ix.
26 Ibid., 41–57.
27 See also Moore, *The Mediation Process*, 187–98.
28 On the role of feelings in family mediation, see Gaughan, 'Divorce and Family Mediation,' 110–17.
29 For a discussion of some difficulties in recognizing diverse interests in family mediation, see Koopman, 'Family Mediation,' 120.

30 Burton, *Conflict and Communication, Deviance, Terrorism and War*, and *Violence Explained*. This overview focuses principally on *Deviance, Terrorism and War*, which presents the major principles that are either taken up or presumed in his other works.

31 Maslow, *Motivation and Personality*, and *Towards a Psychology of Being*.

32 Sites, *Control*.

33 Other needs theorists have offered different lists of human needs; see, e.g., Lederer, Galtung, and Antal, *Human Needs*.

34 See Burton, *Conflict and Communication*; Kelman, 'The Problem-Solving Workshop in Conflict Resolution'; Mitchell and Banks, *Handbook of Conflict Resolution*; and Ronald Fisher, *Interactive Conflict Resolution*.

35 One of the most important theorists of communication is Jürgen Habermas. See *Moral Consciousness and Communicative Action*, in particular, 43–115, and *Between Facts and Norms*, in particular, chaps 7 and 8. See also, Rehg, *Insight and Solidarity*.

36 Pearce, *Communication and the Human Condition*.

37 See, e.g., Mead, *Mind, Self and Society*.

38 See, e.g., Littlejohn and Domenici, *Engaging Communication in Conflict*; and Folger and Jones, *New Directions in Mediation*.

39 Picard, *Mediating*, 18–19. See also Moore, *Mediation Process*; Folberg and Taylor, *Mediation*; Garrett, 'Mediation in Native America'; and Auerbach, *Justice Without Law?*

40 Picard et al., *The Art and Science of Mediation*, xiii, 134–5; Picard, *Mediating*, 18–21.

41 Moore, *Mediation Process*, 14.

42 Ibid., 18.

43 Ibid., 32–3.

44 Picard et al., *The Art and Science of Mediation*, 135–7.

45 Ibid., 41–2.

46 See Kressel, Pruitt, and Associates, *Mediation Research*, 394–402.

47 See Picard et al., *The Art and Science of Mediation*, 112–15.

48 Ibid., 108–10.

49 See Bush and Folger, *The Promise of Mediation*.

50 Ibid., 53–67. See also Picard et al., *The Art and Science of Mediation*, 110–12.

51 Winslade and Monk, *Narrative Mediation*.

52 Picard et al., *The Art and Science of Mediation*, 119–20; Winslade and Monk, *Narrative Mediation*.

53 Picard and Melchin, 'Insight Mediation'; Picard et al., *The Art and Science of Mediation*, 173–83.

54 See our discussion of Insight Mediation in chap. 4.

3 Insight Theory: Transformation through Learning

1　For introductions to Lonergan's method of self-understanding, see Lonergan, *Insight*, introduction and chap. 1, *Method*, chap. 1, 'Method: Trend and Variations,' 'Time and Meaning,' 'The Analogy of Meaning,' and 'Merging Horizons.' See also Melchin, *Living with Other People*; Flanagan, *Quest for Self-Knowledge*; and Crysdale, 'Women and the Social Construction of Self-Appropriation.'
2　On reflective practice, see Schön, *The Reflective Practitioner*.
3　See, e.g., Cranton, *Transformative Learning*, 22–3, 72–7; Mezirow and Associates, *Fostering Critical Reflection*.
4　When we speak of Insight Theory, we are referring to the cognitional theory and method of self-understanding developed by Bernard Lonergan.
5　See Lonergan, *Insight*, chap. 1. See also his, *Verbum*.
6　Some of these observations are reflected in discussions of insight by psychologists. See, e.g., Sternberg and Davidson, *The Nature of Insight*.
7　Lonergan has an interesting discussion of the various patterns of experience, dimensions of meaning, functions of meaning, and differentiations of consciousness in which operations of meaning occur. See Lonergan, *Insight*, chap. 6, and *Method*, chap. 3. See also, 'Time and Meaning,' 'The Analogy of Meaning,' and 'The World Mediated by Meaning.'
8　Lonergan, *Method*, chap. 1. Lonergan uses the term 'judgment' to refer to the group of operations we have called 'verification.'
9　See Lonergan, *Insight*, chap. 1, subsections 2.4 and 2.5, and chap. 9. See also Melchin, *Living with Other People*, 22–7, in particular, 23–4, and 'Moral Decision-Making and the Role of the Moral Question.'
10　On direct insights, see Lonergan, *Insight*, chap. 1. See also McShane, *Wealth of Self*; Flanagan, *Quest for Self-Knowledge*; and Melchin, *Living with Other People*, and *History, Ethics, and Emergent Probability*.
11　On inverse insights, see Lonergan, *Insight*, chap. 1. See also McShane, *Randomness, Statistics and Emergence*, and *Wealth of Self*; Melchin, *History, Ethics, and Emergent Probability*; Flanagan, *Quest for Self-Knowledge*; and Byrne, 'The Thomist Sources of Lonergan's Dynamic World-View.' Lonergan speaks of different kinds of inverse insights: the pure inverse insight (*Insight*, 43–50), the 'devalued' inverse insight involved in statistical inquiry (*Insight*, 78–81), the 'devalued' inverse insight involved in shifts in questioning in common sense (*Insight*, 198–9), and the inverse insight associated with evil (*Insight*, 709, 711). For purposes of introduction throughout this book, we do not differentiate the diverse types; we offer examples of pure inverse insights in these pages, and throughout the book we focus on the occurrence of the third type in conflict.

12 Kuhn, *The Structure of Scientific Revolutions*.

13 See Lonergan, *Insight*, 46–7; Byrne, 'Lonergan on the Foundations of the Theories of Relativity,' in particular, 488. See also Berlinski, *Newton's Gift*, in particular, 34–6.

14 On the transition in science that occurred with Lavoisier, see Kuhn, *Structure*, 52–6. Kuhn articulates clearly this shift in expectations and in questioning that occurs with what Lonergan calls 'inverse insight.' See Lonergan's account of this transition in science in *Phenomenology and Logic*, 111–14. See also Jackson, *A World on Fire*, 135–40.

15 On verification, see Lonergan, *Insight*, chaps 9–13, 'Is it Real?' and 'Philosophical Positions with Regard to Knowing.' Lonergan uses the term 'judgment' to refer to the cognitional operations involved in the verification process. In *Insight*, chap. 10, Lonergan also uses the terms, 'reflective understanding' and 'reflective insight' because verification involves reflecting back on direct and inverse insights and asking whether or not they are correct, whether they can be verified by the evidence.

16 For introductions to some of these discussions, see, e.g., Meynell, *Redirecting Philosophy*; McCarthy, *The Crisis of Philosophy*; Fitzpatrick, *Philosophical Encounters*; and Kanaris and Doorley, *In Deference to the Other*.

17 On feelings and values, see Lonergan, *Insight*, chaps 6, 7, 18, *Method*, chap. 2, 'Horizons,' 'What Are Judgments of Value?' and 'The Human Good.' See also Melchin, 'Ethics in Insight,' and *Living with Other People*; Crowe, 'An Exploration of Lonergan's New Notion of Value,' and 'An Expansion of Lonergan's New Notion of Value'; and Doorley, *The Place of the Heart in Lonergan's Ethics*.

18 The Transformative Mediation model has this focus on moral development. See, Bush and Folger, *The Promise of Mediation*, chap. 9.

4 Insight Mediation: Applying Insight Theory to Mediation

1 For a fuller overview of the history of conflict studies, see chapter 2.

2 For introductions to the mediation model practised and taught at Carleton University, see Picard, *Mediating*, and Picard et al., *The Art and Science of Mediation*. For on-line resources on mediation at Carleton, see http://www.carleton.ca/ccer.

3 See Melchin, *Living with Other People*, and *History, Ethics, and Emergent Probability*. Researchers at Saint Paul University have applied Lonergan's work to the fields of ethics, health care, economics, and conflict. See Melchin, 'Moral Knowledge and the Structure of Cooperative Living'; Doucet, Larouche, and Melchin, *Ethical Deliberation in Multiprofessional Health Care Teams*; and Melchin, 'Economies, Ethics, and the Structure of Social Living,'

and 'Pluralism, Conflict, and the Structure of the Public Good.' For on-line resources, see http://www.ustpaul.ca/Lonergancentre.

4 See chapter 1 of this book for a discussion of how we build upon and develop the Transformative Learning Theory of Jack Mezirow.

5 On Insight Mediation, see Picard and Melchin, 'Insight Mediation'; and Picard, 'Learning about Learning.' On the steps of the mediation process, see Picard and Melchin, 'Insight Mediation,' 38–40; Picard et al., *The Art and Science of Mediation*, 173–83; and Picard, *Mediating*, 101–13.

6 See Picard and Melchin, 'Insight Mediation,' 40–1.

7 On Lonergan's idea of 'horizons,' see his *Method*, 77, 220–4, 235–7, 'Horizons,' and 'Horizons and Transpositions.' See also Melchin, *Living with Other People*, 27–31.

8 The case of 'Danny and Teresa' was the mediation roleplay we videotaped and analysed to discover and develop the Insight Mediation model.

9 See the discussion of feelings and values in Lonergan in chapter 3 of this book.

10 The mediator strategy of 'de-linking' is discussed in greater detail later in this chapter.

5 Insight, Conflict, and Justice: Two Case Studies

1 For discussions of restorative justice approaches that critically assess the justice system and focus on the needs of victims, families, and communities, see Zehr, *Changing Lenses*; Wright and Galaway, *Mediation and Criminal Justice*; Sharpe, *Restorative Justice*; and Van Ness and Strong, *Restoring Justice*.

2 See Church Council on Justice and Corrections, *Satisfying Justice*; and Scott, 'Collaborative Justice Project's Learning Profiled to the Ontario Office for Victims of Crime Conference.' See also the references in note 1, above.

3 Church Council on Justice and Corrections, 'Elizabeth's Story: Victim of Armed Robbery.' This case came from Wendy Keats of MOVE Inc., an organization in New Brunswick, Canada, devoted to victim-offender mediations.

4 Church Council on Justice and Corrections, 'The Story of Regina v. Philip Moses.'

6 Concluding Reflections

1 See Jacobs, *The Death and Life of Great American Cities*, *The Economy of Cities*, *Cities and the Wealth of Nations*, *Systems of Survival*, *The Nature of Economies*, and *Dark Age Ahead*.

2 On the links between the works of Jane Jacobs and Lonergan, see Lawrence, *Ethics in Making a Living*. For a discussion of the role of insight throughout Jacobs's work, see his editor's introduction, in *Ethics in Making a Living*, iii–vii. See also his 'Response to "Systems of Economic Ethics"'; and Byrne, 'Jane Jacobs and the Common Good.'

3 For a discussion of alternative approaches to democracy, see Melchin, 'Reaching Toward Democracy.'

4 For an excellent discussion of this problem, see Taylor, *The Malaise of Modernity*. This text is published in the United States as *The Ethics of Authenticity*. See also Taylor, *Sources of the Self*.

5 For a critical analysis of diverse ways of understanding toleration, see Walzer, *On Toleration*.

6 Cohen, 'Procedure and Substance in Deliberative Democracy,' and 'Deliberation and Democratic Legitimacy'; Habermas, 'Three Normative Models,' and 'Popular Sovereignty as Procedure.' See also Benhabib, 'Toward a Deliberative Model'; and Bohman, 'Deliberative Democracy and Effective Social Freedom.'

7 Habermas, 'Popular Sovereignty as Procedure,' 55–60. See also Rehg, *Insight and Solidarity*, 56–83; and Habermas, *Moral Consciousness*, in particular, 43–115, and *Between Facts and Norms*, in particular, chaps. 7 and 8.

Bibliography

On-Line Resources

http://www.bc.edu/bc_org/avp/cas/lonergan
http://www.carleton.ca/ccer
http://lonergan.concordia.ca
http://www.lonergan-lri.ca/index1.shtml
http://www.shu.edu/catholic-mission/lonergan
http://www.ustpaul.ca/lonergancentre

Books and Articles

Anderson, Bruce. *Discovery in Legal Decision-Making*. Dordrecht: Kluwer, 1996.
Auerbach, J.S. *Justice Without Law? Resolving Disputes Without Lawyers*. New York: Oxford University Press, 1983.
Axelrod, Robert. *The Evolution of Cooperation*. New York: Basic Books, 1994.
Benhabib, Seyla, ed. *Democracy and Difference: Contesting the Boundaries of the Political*. Princeton, NJ: Princeton University Press, 1996.
– 'Toward a Deliberative Model of Democratic Legitimacy.' In *Democracy and Difference*, ed. Benhabib, 67–94.
Berger, Peter. *Invitation to Sociology: A Humanistic Perspective*. New York: Doubleday, 1963.
Bergmann, Thomas J., and Roger J. Volkema. 'Understanding and Managing Interpersonal Conflict at Work: Its Issues, Interactive Processes, and Consequences.' In *Managing Conflict: An Interdisciplinary Approach*, ed. M. Afzalur Rahim, 7–19. New York: Praeger, 1989.
Berlinski, David. *Newton's Gift: How Sir Isaac Newton Unlocked the System of the World*. New York: Free Press, 2000.

Bohman, James. 'Deliberative Democracy and Effective Social Freedom: Capabilities, Resources, and Opportunities.' In *Deliberative Democracy*, ed. Bohman and Rehg, 321–48.

Bohman, James, and William Rehg, eds. *Deliberative Democracy: Essays on Reason and Politics*. Cambridge, MA: MIT Press, 1997.

Boulding, Kenneth. Foreword. In *Conflict Management and Problem Solving: Interpersonal to International Applications*, ed. Dennis J.D. Sandole and Ingrid Sandole-Staroste, ix–x. New York: New York University Press, 1987.

Braman, Brian J. *Meaning and Authenticity: Bernard Lonergan and Charles Taylor on the Drama of Authentic Human Existence*. Toronto: University of Toronto Press, 2008.

Burton, John W. *Conflict and Communication: The Use of Controlled Communication in International Relations*. London: Macmillan; New York: Free Press, 1969.

– *Deviance, Terrorism and War: The Process of Solving Unsolved Social and Political Problems*. New York: St Martin's Press, 1979.

– *Violence Explained: The Sources of Conflict, Violence and Crime and Their Provention*. Manchester and New York: Manchester University Press, 1997.

– *World Society*. London: Cambridge University Press, 1972.

Bush, Robert A. Baruch, and Joseph P. Folger. *The Promise of Mediation: Responding to Conflict Through Empowerment and Recognition*. San Francisco: Jossey-Bass, 1994.

– *The Promise of Mediation: The Transformative Approach to Conflict*. San Francisco: Jossey-Bass, 2005.

Byrne, Patrick. 'Jane Jacobs and the Common Good.' In *Ethics in Making a Living*, ed. Lawrence, 169–89.

– 'Lonergan on the Foundations of the Theories of Relativity.' In *Creativity and Method: Essays in Honor of Bernard Lonergan*, ed. Matthew Lamb, 477–94. Milwaukee: Marquette University Press, 1981.

– 'The Thomist Sources of Lonergan's Dynamic World-View.' *The Thomist* 46 (1982): 108–45.

Church Council on Justice and Corrections. 'Elizabeth's Story: Victim of Armed Robbery.' Case on file. Ottawa: Church Council on Justice and Corrections, accessed 2005. www.ccjc.ca.

Church Council on Justice and Corrections. *Satisfying Justice*. Ottawa: Church Council on Justice and Corrections, 1996. www.ccjc.ca.

Church Council on Justice and Corrections. 'The Story of Regina v. Philip Moses.' Case on file. Ottawa: Church Council on Justice and Corrections, accessed 2005. Original case transcripts indexed as *R. v. Moses* [1992] 3 C.N.L.R.116, Yukon Territorial Court, Stuart J.

Cohen, Joshua. 'Deliberation and Democratic Legitimacy.' In *Deliberative Democracy*, ed. Bohman and Rehg, 67–91.

– 'Procedure and Substance in Deliberative Democracy.' In *Democracy and Difference*, ed. Benhabib, 95–119.

Coser, Lewis A. *Continuities in the Study of Social Conflict*. New York: Free Press, 1968.

– *The Functions of Social Conflict*. New York: Free Press, 1956.

Cranton, Patricia. *Understanding and Promoting Transformative Learning: A Guide for Educators of Adults*. San Francisco: Jossey-Bass, 1994.

Crowe, Frederick E. 'An Expansion of Lonergan's New Notion of Value.' In *Appropriating the Lonergan Idea*, ed. M. Vertin, 344–59. Washington, DC: Catholic University of America Press, 1989.

– 'An Exploration of Lonergan's New Notion of Value.' In *Appropriating the Lonergan Idea*, ed. M. Vertin, 51–70. Washington, DC: Catholic University of America Press, 1989.

Crysdale, Cynthia S.W., ed. *Lonergan and Feminism*. Toronto: University of Toronto Press, 1994.

– 'Women and the Social Construction of Self-Appropriation.' In *Lonergan and Feminism*, ed. Crysdale, 88–113.

Deutsch, Morton. 'A Theoretical Perspective on Conflict and Conflict Resolution.' In *Conflict Management and Problem Solving*, ed. Sandole and Sandole-Staroste, 38–49.

Doorley, Mark J. *The Place of the Heart in Lonergan's Ethics: The Role of Feelings in the Ethical Intentionality Analysis of Bernard Lonergan*. Lanham, MD: University Press of America, 1996.

Doucet, Hubert, Jean-Marc Larouche, and Kenneth R. Melchin, eds. *Ethical Deliberation in Multiprofessional Health Care Teams*. Ottawa: University of Ottawa Press, 2001.

Elias, John, and Sharan Merriam. *Philosophical Foundations of Adult Education*. Huntington, NY: Robert E. Krieger, 1980.

Finger, Matthias, and José Manuel Asún. *Adult Education at the Crossroads: Learning Our Way Out*. London: Zed Books, 2001.

Fisher, Roger, and William Ury. *Getting to Yes: Negotiating Agreement Without Giving In*. Ed. Bruce Patton. Harmondsworth: Penguin Books, 1981.

Fisher, Ronald. *Interactive Conflict Resolution*. Syracuse, NY: Syracuse University Press, 1997.

Fitzpatrick, Joseph P. *Philosophical Encounters: Lonergan and the Analytic Tradition*. Toronto: University of Toronto Press, 2005.

Flanagan, Joseph. *Quest for Self-Knowledge: An Essay in Lonergan's Philosophy*. Toronto: University of Toronto Press, 1997.

Folberg, Jay, and Alison Taylor. *Mediation: A Comprehensive Guide to Resolving Conflict*. San Francisco: Jossey-Bass, 1984.

Folger, Joseph P., and Tricia Jones, eds. *New Directions in Mediation: Communication Research and Perspectives*. Thousand Oaks, CA: Sage, 1994.

Garrett, R.D. 'Mediation in Native America.' *Dispute Resolution Journal* 49 (1994): 38–45.

Gaughan, Lawrence D. 'Divorce and Family Mediation.' In *Conflict Management and Problem Solving*, ed. Sandole and Sandole-Staroste, 107–18.

Giddens, Anthony. *New Rules of Sociological Method: A Positive Critique of Interpretative Sociologies*. London: Hutchinson, 1976.

Habermas, Jürgen. *Between Facts and Norms: Contributions to a Discourse Theory of Law and Democracy*. Trans. William Rehg. Cambridge, MA: MIT Press, 1996. First published 1992.

– *Moral Consciousness and Communicative Action*. Trans. C. Lenhardt and S. Weber Nicholsen. Cambridge, MA: MIT Press, 1990. First published 1983.

– 'Popular Sovereignty as Procedure.' In *Deliberative Democracy*, ed. Bohman and Rehg, 35–65.

– 'Three Normative Models of Democracy.' In *Democracy and Difference*, ed. Benhabib, 21–30.

Hegel, Georg Wilhelm Friedrich. *Lectures on the Philosophy of World History: Introduction: Reason in History*. Trans. H. Nisbet, with an introduction by D. Forbes. Cambridge: Cambridge University Press, 1975.

Hobbes, Thomas. *Leviathan*. 1651. Ed. Michael Oakeshott. New York: Collier Books, 1977.

Jackson, Joe. *A World on Fire: A Heretic, an Aristocrat, and the Race to Discover Oxygen*. New York: Viking, 2005.

Jacobs, Jane. *Cites and the Wealth of Nations: Principles of Economic Life*. New York: Vintage Books, 1985.

– *Dark Age Ahead*. New York: Random House Canada, 2004.

– *The Death and Life of Great American Cities*. New York: Vintage Books, 1961.

– *The Economy of Cities*. New York: Vintage Books, 1970.

– *The Nature of Economies*. New York: Modern Library, 2000.

– *Systems of Survival: A Dialogue on the Moral Foundations of Commerce and Politics*. New York: Vintage Books, 1994.

Kanaris, Jim, and Mark Doorley, eds. *In Deference to the Other: Lonergan and Contemporary Continental Thought*. Albany: SUNY Press, 2004.

Kelman, Herbert. 'The Problem-Solving Workshop in Conflict Resolution.' *Journal of Peace Research* 13 (1976): 79–90.

Koopman, Elizabeth Janssen. 'Family Mediation: A Developmental Perspective on the Field.' In *Conflict Management and Problem Solving*, ed. Sandole and Sandole-Staroste, 119–29.

Kremenyuk, Victor A. 'The Emerging System of International Negotiation.' In *International Negotiation*, ed. Kremenyuk, 22–39.

– ed. *International Negotiation: Analysis, Approaches, Issues*. San Francisco: Jossey-Bass, 1991.

Kressel, Kenneth, Dean G. Pruitt, and Associates. *Mediation Research: The Process and Effectiveness of Third-Party Intervention*. San Francisco: Jossey-Bass, 1989.

Kuhn, Thomas S. *The Structure of Scientific Revolutions*. 3rd ed. Chicago: University of Chicago Press, 1996.

Lamb, Matthew, ed. *Creativity and Method: Essays in Honor of Bernard Lonergan*. Milwaukee, WI: Marquette University Press, 1981.

Lawrence, Fred, ed. *Ethics in Making a Living: The Jane Jacobs Conference*. Atlanta, GA: Scholars Press, 1989.

– 'The Fragility of Consciousness: Lonergan and the Postmodern Concern for the Other.' *Theological Studies* 54 (1993): 55–94.

– 'Response to "Systems of Economic Ethics."' In *Ethics in Making a Living*, ed. Lawrence, 191–96.

Lederer, Katrin, Johan Galtung, and David Antal, eds. *Human Needs: A Contribution to the Current Debate*. Cambridge, MA: Oelgeschlanger, Gunn & Hain, 1980.

Littlejohn, Stephen W., and Kathy Domenici. *Engaging Communication in Conflict: Systemic Practice*. Thousand Oaks, CA: Sage, 2001.

Lonergan, Bernard. 'The Analogy of Meaning.' In *Philosophical and Theological Papers 1958–1964*, 183–213.

– 'Horizons.' In *Philosophical and Theological Papers 1965–1980*, 10–29.

– 'Horizons and Transpositions.' In *Philosophical and Theological Papers 1965–1980*, 409–32.

– 'The Human Good.' In *Philosophical and Theological Papers 1965–1980*, 332–51.

– *Insight: A Study of Human Understanding*. Ed. Frederick E. Crowe and Robert M. Doran. Vol. 3 of Collected Works of Bernard Lonergan. Toronto: University of Toronto Press, 1992. First published 1957.

– 'Is It Real?' In *Philosophical and Theological Papers 1965–1980*, 119–39.

– 'Merging Horizons: System, Common Sense, Scholarship.' In *Philosophical and Theological Papers 1965–1980*, 49–69.

– *Method in Theology*. Toronto: University of Toronto Press, 1990. First published 1972.

– 'Method: Trend and Variations.' In *A Third Collection*, 13–22.

– *Phenomenology and Logic: The Boston College Lectures on Mathematical Logic and Existentialism*. Ed. Philip J. McShane. Vol. 18 of Collected Works of Bernard Lonergan. Toronto: University of Toronto Press, 2001.

– *Philosophical and Theological Papers 1958–1964*. Ed. Robert C. Croken, Freder-

ick E. Crowe, and Robert M. Doran. Vol. 6 of Collected Works of Bernard
Lonergan. Toronto: University of Toronto Press, 1996.
- *Philosophical and Theological Papers 1965–1980*. Ed. Robert C. Croken and Rob-
ert M. Doran. Vol. 17 of Collected Works of Bernard Lonergan. Toronto: Uni-
versity of Toronto Press, 1996.
- 'Philosophical Positions with Regard to Knowing.' In *Philosophical and Theo-
logical Papers 1958–1964*, 214–43.
- *A Third Collection: Papers by Bernard J.F. Lonergan, S.J.* Ed. Frederick E. Crowe.
Mahwah, NJ: Paulist Press, 1985.
- 'Time and Meaning.' In *Philosophical and Theological Papers 1958–1964*, 94–
121.
- *Topics in Education*. Ed. Frederick E. Crowe. Vol. 10 of Collected Works of Ber-
nard Lonergan. Toronto: University of Toronto Press, 1993.
- *Understanding and Being: The Halifax Lectures on Insight*. Ed. Frederick E.
Crowe, Robert M. Doran, Thomas V. Daly, Elizabeth A. Morelli, and Mark D.
Morelli. Vol. 5 of Collected Works of Bernard Lonergan. Toronto: University
of Toronto Press, 1996.
- *Verbum: Word and Idea in Aquinas*. Ed. Frederick E. Crowe and Robert M.
Doran. Vol. 2 of Collected Works of Bernard Lonergan. Toronto: University
of Toronto Press, 1997.
- 'What Are Judgments of Value?' In *Philosophical and Theological Papers 1965–
1980*, 140–56.
- 'The World Mediated by Meaning.' In *Philosophical and Theological Papers
1965–1980*, 107–18.
Marsick, Victoria J. 'Action Learning and Reflection in the Workplace.' In *Fos-
tering Critical Reflection in Adulthood*, by Mezirow and Associates, 23–46.
Marx, Karl. 'Economic and Philosophic Manuscripts of 1844.' In *The Marx-
Engels Reader*, 2nd ed. Ed. Robert Tucker. Trans. M. Milligan. New York: W.W.
Norton, 1978.
Maslow, Abraham H. *Motivation and Personality.* 3rd ed. New York: Harper and
Row, 1987. First published 1954.
- *Towards a Psychology of Being*. New York: Van Nostrand, 1968.
Mathews, William A. *Lonergan's Quest: A Study of Desire in the Authoring of
Insight*. Toronto: University of Toronto Press, 2005.
McCarthy, Michael H. *The Crisis of Philosophy.* Albany: SUNY Press, 1989.
McShane, Philip. *Randomness, Statistics and Emergence*. Dublin: Gill and Mac-
millan, 1970.
- *Wealth of Self and Wealth of Nations: Self-Axis of the Great Ascent*. Washington,
DC: University Press of America, 1981.
Mead, George Herbert. *Mind, Self and Society: From the Standpoint of a Social*

Behaviorist. Ed. Charles W. Morris. Chicago: University of Chicago Press, 1962. First published 1934.

Meadows, Donella H., Dennis L. Meadows, Jørgen Randers, and William W. Behrens III. *Limits to Growth*. 2nd ed. New York: Universe Books, 1975.

Melchin, Kenneth R. 'Economies, Ethics, and the Structure of Social Living.' *Humanomics* 10 (1994): 21–57.

– 'Ethics in Insight.' In *Lonergan Workshop*. Vol. 8. Ed. Fred Lawrence, 135–47. Atlanta, GA: Scholars Press, 1990.

– *History, Ethics, and Emergent Probability: Ethics, Society, and History in the Work of Bernard Lonergan*. 2nd ed. Ottawa: The Lonergan Website, 1999.

– *Living with Other People: An Introduction to Christian Ethics Based on Bernard Lonergan*. Ottawa: Novalis; Collegeville, MN: Liturgical Press, 1998.

– 'Moral Decision-Making and the Role of the Moral Question.' *Method: Journal of Lonergan Studies* 11 (1993): 215–28.

– 'Pluralism, Conflict, and the Structure of the Public Good.' In *The Promise of Critical Theology: Essays in Honour of Charles Davis*, ed. Marc Lalonde, 75–92. Waterloo: Wilfred Laurier University Press, 1995.

– 'Reaching toward Democracy: Theology and Theory When Talk Turns to War.' *Catholic Theological Society of America, Proceedings* 58 (2003): 41–59.

Merriam, Sharan, and Rosemary S. Caffarella. *Learning in Adulthood: A Comprehensive Guide*. 2nd ed. San Francisco: Jossey-Bass, 1999.

Meynell, Hugo A. *Introduction to the Philosophy of Bernard Lonergan*. 2nd ed. Toronto: University of Toronto Press, 1991.

– *Redirecting Philosophy: Reflections on the Nature of Knowledge from Plato to Lonergan*. Toronto: University of Toronto Press, 1998.

Mezirow, Jack. 'How Critical Reflection Triggers Transformative Learning.' In *Fostering Critical Reflection in Adulthood*, by Mezirow and Associates, 1–20.

Mezirow, Jack, and Associates. *Fostering Critical Reflection in Adulthood: A Guide to Transformative and Emancipatory Learning*. San Francisco: Jossey-Bass, 1990.

Mitchell, Christopher, and Michael Banks. *Handbook of Conflict Resolution: The Analytical Problem-Solving Approach*. New York: Pinter, 1996.

Moore, Christopher W. *The Mediation Process: Practical Strategies for Resolving Conflict*. San Francisco: Jossey-Bass, 1986.

Pearce, Barnett W. *Communication and the Human Condition*. Carbondale, IL: Southern Illinois University, 1989.

Picard, Cheryl A. 'Learning about Learning: The Value of "Insight."' *Conflict Resolution Quarterly* 20 (2003): 477–84.

– *Mediating Interpersonal and Small Group Conflict*. Rev. ed. Ottawa: Golden Dog Press, 2002.

Picard, Cheryl A., Peter Bishop, Rena Ramkay, and Neil Sargent. *The Art and Science of Mediation*. Toronto: Emond Montgomery, 2004.

Picard, Cheryl A., and Kenneth R. Melchin. 'Insight Mediation: A Learning-Centered Mediation Model.' *Negotiation Journal* 23 (2007): 35–53.

Rahim, M. Afzalur, ed. *Managing Conflict: An Interdisciplinary Approach*. New York: Praeger, 1989.

Raiffa, Howard. *The Art and Science of Negotiation: How to Resolve Conflicts and Get the Best out of Bargaining*. Cambridge, MA: Harvard University Press, 1982.

– 'Contributions of Applied Systems Analysis to International Negotiation.' In *International Negotiation*, ed. Kremenyuk, 5–21.

Rehg, William. *Insight and Solidarity: A Study in the Discourse Ethics of Jürgen Habermas*. Berkeley, CA: University of California Press, 1994.

Sandole, Dennis J.D., and Ingrid Sandole-Staroste, eds. *Conflict Management and Problem Solving: Interpersonal to International Applications*. New York: New York University Press, 1987.

Schön, Donald A. *The Reflective Practitioner: How Professionals Think in Action*. New York: Basic Books, 1983.

Scott, James. 'Collaborative Justice Project's Learning Profiled to the Ontario Office for Victims of Crime Conference.' Ottawa: Church Council on Justice and Corrections, 2005. Accessed 25 April 2007 at http://www.ccjc.ca/currentissues/victims/collaborativejustice.html.

Sharpe, Susan. *Restorative Justice: A Vision for Healing and Change*. Edmonton, AB: Edmonton Victim Offender Mediation Society, 1998.

Siebe, Wilfried. 'Game Theory.' In *International Negotiation*, ed. Kremenyuk, 180–202.

Sites, Paul. *Control: The Basis of Social Order*. New York: Dunellen, 1973.

Sternberg, R., and J. Davidson, eds. *The Nature of Insight*. Cambridge, MA: MIT Press, 1995.

Taylor, Charles. *The Ethics of Authenticity*. Cambridge, MA: Harvard University Press, 1992.

– *Malaise of Modernity*. Concord, ON: House of Anansi Press, 1991.

– *Sources of the Self: The Making of the Modern Identity*. Cambridge, MA: Harvard University Press, 1989.

Tjosvold, Dean. 'Interdependence Approach to Conflict Management in Organizations.' In *Managing Conflict*, ed. Rahim, 41–50.

– Introduction. In *Managing Conflict*, ed. Rahim, 3–6.

Van Ness, Daniel W., and Karen Heetderks Strong. *Restoring Justice*. Cincinnati, OH: Anderson, 1997.

von Neumann, John, and Oskar Morgenstern. *Theory of Games and Economic Behaviour*. Princeton, NJ: Princeton University Press, 1944.

Walzer, Michael. *On Toleration*. New Haven, CT: Yale University Press, 1997.

Wedge, Bryant. Introduction. In *Conflict Management and Problem Solving*, ed. Sandole and Sandole-Staroste, 1–2.

Winslade, John, and Gerald Monk. *Narrative Mediation*. San Francisco: Jossey-Bass, 2000.

Wolin, Sheldon S. 'Fugitive Democracy.' In *Democracy and Difference*, ed. Benhabib, 31–45.

Wright, Martin, and Burt Galaway, eds. *Mediation and Criminal Justice: Victims, Offenders, and Community*. London: Sage, 1989.

Young, Iris Marion. 'Communication and the Other: Beyond Deliberative Democracy.' In *Democracy and Difference*, ed. Benhabib, 120–35.

– 'Difference as a Resource for Democratic Communication.' In *Deliberative Democracy*, ed. Bohman and Rehg, 383–406.

– *Throwing Like a Girl and Other Essays in Feminist Philosophy and Social Theory*. Bloomington: Indiana University Press, 1990.

Zehr, Howard. *Changing Lenses*. Scottdale, PA: Herald Press, 1990.

Index